IMAGES
of America

BLACK ROCK DESERT

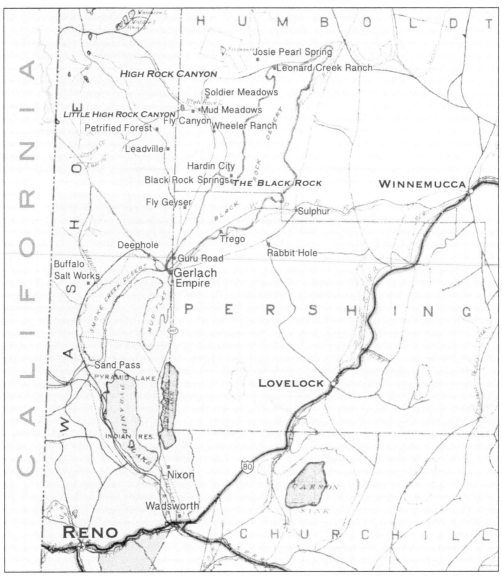

This map of the Black Rock Desert area—based on a 1919 road map of Nevada from the Mary B. Ansari Map Library at the University of Nevada, Reno—includes locations discussed in the text. (Illustration by Tansy Brooks.)

ON THE COVER: The Thumb, located at Fly Ranch, about 24 miles north of Gerlach, is a travertine formation that emerged in 1914 when a well was being drilled. Louis Gerlach's son Fred homesteaded Fly Ranch in the late 1800s. The springs near Fly Ranch were referred to as Ward's Hot Springs in an 1886 geology report. (University Archives, University of Nevada-Reno, Jay A. Carpenter Collection, 88-55-1095.)

IMAGES
of America

BLACK ROCK DESERT

Christopher Brooks

ARCADIA
PUBLISHING

Published by Arcadia Publishing
Charleston, South Carolina

Library of Congress Control Number: 2013950889

For all general information, please contact Arcadia Publishing:
Telephone 843-853-2070
Fax 843-853-0044
E-mail sales@arcadiapublishing.com
For customer service and orders:
Toll-Free 1-888-313-2665

Visit us on the Internet at www.arcadiapublishing.com

This book is dedicated to Bev Osborn.

All of the author's proceeds from this book are being
donated to the Gerlach Senior Citizen Center, which
provides lunch to Black Rock Desert seniors.

CONTENTS

FOREWORD

A late afternoon drive on the Black Rock Desert. You drive northward for miles across the largest flat expanse of desert in North America, a cloud of alkali dust billowing behind you. Finally you reach what appears to be the middle, though the playa is so vast that it is hard to determine, with Trego Peak to the east, the black rock after which the desert is named and the Calicos to the north and northwest, and far to the northeast the summit of King Lear Peak.

You stop, turn off the engine, let the dust settle, and step out of your vehicle. A silence surrounds you, more profound than any other silence you have known, and the air is clear and crisp as your mind is emptied of all extraneous thoughts as you listen to the soft tick of your engine cooling down. This spot feels as good as any, and you walk away from your vehicle to take in the vastness of your home for the night, the shadow of your body lengthening on the playa as the sun begins to lower behind the Granite Range far to the west, clouds gathering and flaring above the peaks.

You return to your vehicle, take a folded, eight-inch foam pad the size of a double bed from the trunk, and lay it on a tarp, making it up with sheets, blankets, and pillows as the air grows noticeably cooler with each passing minute. You take a bottle of cold spring water from your cooler, some bread and cheese, an orange or two, a bar of chocolate, and set them by your bed. That is all it takes.

You have a long, deep swallow of water and lay down on your bed, your head on the pillows, and look deep into space as twilight fades and the stars come out, one by one, on the dark velvet curtain of a moonless night, so bright you can see the star shadow of your hand on the desert floor as you lift it into the cool, clear air. Are you looking up or down? It does not matter. The Milky Way arches overhead in a bridge of dreams between this world and that. Home at last.

—Michael Sykes

ACKNOWLEDGMENTS

I would like to thank Don Asher for introducing me to the Black Rock Desert in the late 1980s and for setting a good example about how to develop a book. Special thanks go to Michael Sykes for writing the foreword and believing that I could do the job. This book would be empty without the contributions of photographs from many people, including Kevin Allec (Vera Haviland's grandson), John Bogard, Tansy Brooks, Gus Bundy, Cindy Carter, Sunny DeForest, R'Deen Diebold, Tony Diebold, Melissa Edgecomb, Karen Fiene, Basil Galloway, Peter Goin, Douglas Keister, Patricia Kelley, Robert Lind, Mel Lyons, Jeff Manos, Lorie Manos (Henry Lind's grandniece), James T. Neal, Jeff Pringle, David Rumsey, and Patricia Speelman. I would like to thank my reviewers, including John Bogard, Robert Brooks, Cindy Carter, Sunny DeForest, Karen Fiene, Patricia Kelley, Mel Lyons, Patricia Speelman, and Mary Stewart. Any errors or omissions are mine.

I would also like to acknowledge the help of professional librarians and historians Lee Brumbaugh, Phillip I. Earl, and Heidi Englund at the Nevada Historical Society; Donnelyn Curtis, Jessica Maddox, Kimberley Roberts, and Jacquelyn K. Sundstrand at the University of Nevada, Reno; Dana Toth at the Humboldt Museum; George Thompson at California State University, Chico; and Kelli Luchs, at the University of Nevada, Las Vegas.

When I started this project, I had no idea how important the moral support of my family would be, so I would like to thank Tansy Brooks, Lauren Winter, and Basil Galloway.

INTRODUCTION

The Black Rock Desert, located in northwestern Nevada, has been the site of human activities ranging from ancient hunters to the arrival of the pioneers to present-day motion pictures, land speed records, commercial photography, and a weeklong art festival.

The definition of the Black Rock Desert varies among individuals. Typically, the name Black Rock Desert refers to the 200-square-mile dry lakebed located about 100 miles north of Reno, Nevada, near the town of Gerlach. The large flat expanse of the dry lakebed is what attracts many visitors to the region. Many know this area as the Playa. The word *playa* comes from the Spanish word for beach. Locally, the term *playa* refers to a dry lakebed. A more general definition of the Black Rock Desert includes the northeast arm, which consists of sagebrush and small playas. The US Geological Survey defines the 11,600-square-mile Black Rock Desert watershed as including an area from the Smoke Creek Desert to the south up to small portions of California and Oregon to the northeast. This book focuses on the history of the region up until 1990, primarily using images of the main dry lakebed of the Black Rock Desert and the small town of Gerlach.

The desert is named for Black Rock Point, which early pioneers used on the Applegate-Lassen Trail as they crossed from Rabbit Hole Springs on their way to southern Oregon. Evidence of mammoths and other large mammals have been recovered from the area. In 1979, the tooth of a mammoth was found in the northeastern arm of the desert. Material found near this mammoth has been dated to between 15,000 and 17,000 years of age. The bones that were later recovered were deemed too fragile for display, so casts were made and the results were put on display in 1993 at the Nevada State Museum in Carson City.

The Black Rock Desert was covered by ancient Lake Lahontan. At the lake's peak, 12,700 years ago, the Black Rock Desert was under about 500 feet of water. By about 9,000 years ago, Lake Lahontan had nearly dried up; the stages of drying are visible today as bathtub ring–like terraces that appear on the ridges surrounding the area. Today, the remains of Lake Lahontan include Pyramid Lake and Winnemucca Lake, located just south of the Black Rock Desert. In 2013, researchers determined that petroglyphs at Winnemucca Lake were created by human visitors between 14,800 and 10,500 years ago, making them the oldest known petroglyphs in North America. The earliest evidence of humans in the Black Rock Desert dates to about 5,000 years ago, in the form of arrowheads found near the current shore of the Black Rock Desert playa.

In late 1843, John C. Frémont entered the area from the north, traveling through High Rock Canyon and visiting Black Rock Hot Springs. In 1846, Jesse and Lindsay Applegate created a trail to southern Oregon using Frémont's route. Peter Lassen then created a trail—known as the Lassen Cutoff—that led through the area and toward the California gold country. The 1848 gold finds in California brought a number of pioneers through the area, though the route added 200 long, hard miles over the more southerly route that passed through the Forty Mile Desert east of present-day Fernley, Nevada. A portion of the trail between Rabbit Hole Springs and the Black Rock Desert was 21 miles, usually with no water. An account mentions 82 dead oxen, two dead horses, and one dead mule near Rabbit Hole Springs. In 1859, Peter Lassen and Edward Clapper were murdered north of Black Rock Point. Legend has it that the murders were revenge for spreading misleading information about the conditions of the trail, though evidence points to the murderer being their companion Americus Wyatt. In 1856, William Nobles created a trail from the Black Rock Desert south through the Smoke Creek Desert to California.

In the late 1800s, Louis Gerlach purchased a number of ranches to create the Gerlach Land and Livestock Company, where cattle were driven up to 200 miles to the nearest railhead in Reno.

Between 1905 and 1909, the Western Pacific Railroad built a portion of tracks in the area coming from the Feather River in California, passing just south of the dry lakebed, and heading east to Winnemucca. The town of Gerlach was settled in 1906 and adopted the name from that of the Gerlach Land and Livestock Company. The city established a post office in 1909, and Western Pacific built a roundhouse and water tower. The town lots were owned by the railroad, and in 1975, the entire town (including the water system) was sold to the residents for $18,000.

In 1910, gypsum was found about 10 miles south of the playa and was mined from about the 1920s until 2011, first by the Pacific Portland Cement Company and then by US Gypsum. The company-owned town of Empire, Nevada, was established in 1923 and boasted its own airstrip, nine-hole golf course, and post office.

In 1926, *The Winning of Barbara Worth* was filmed on the east side of the dry lakebed; a siding was added at Trego for the film crew to use. This silent film stars Ronald Colman and Vilma Bánky, as well as Gary Cooper in his first title role. The Black Rock Desert appears in other movies, such as the 1989 Drew Barrymore/Matt Frewer film *Far from Home*.

After Louis Gerlach's death, Ed Waltz bought the property and ran it as the Gerlach and Waltz Ranch. Lawrence Holland eventually bought the property and purchased other ranches. When Holland sold the land in 1952, the sale of one million acres was reported as being 25 percent larger than the state of Rhode Island. The land, at $3 per acre, was thought to be the largest piece of private property ever sold in the United States.

The Black Rock Desert was used as a military aerial gunnery range from 1945 until at least 1959. During that time, planes from Fallon Naval Air Station and Alameda Naval Air Station would practice with .50 caliber and 22-millimeter machine guns. The area was not formally used as a bombing range, though the remains of many types of ordnance have been found.

During the 1950s, interest increased in ghost towns and deserts. *Desert Magazine* features a number of articles by Nell Murbarger that cover topics such as Hardin City, site of a silver rush in the 1860s; Jose Pearl, a longtime resident of the area; and the Navy's aerial gunnery range.

The 1960s found people visiting the area for the hot springs, discovering the unique beauty of the area, and then pursuing artistic endeavors. In 1968, Michael Heizer created a series of land art installations in Nevada and California, one of which was created on the lakebed and was featured in *Life* magazine. Over time, other artists have used the area for both artistic and commercial photography, especially automobile advertisements.

In the 1970s, local artists were using the desert as a medium. Gerlach resident DeWayne "Dooby" Williams started Guru Road (aka Dooby Lane), which consists of roughly one mile of sculptures that use regional material and features aphorisms carved into local rocks.

Sessions S. Wheeler's 1978 book *The Black Rock Desert* describes the history of the area in detail. While researching his book, Wheeler took many photographs. A few of his images are included in this book.

In the 1980s, Mel Lyons (from the San Francisco area) and John Bogard (from Gerlach) hosted a series of events, including "Croquet X Machina"—a croquet game played with croquet balls almost six feet in diameter that were hit with trucks. Another event put on by Lyons and Bogard was "Ya Gotta Regatta—The Breakwind Dance," for which each attendee created an art piece, many of which were wind-based. Photographer Douglas Keister (then from Emeryville, California) started a golf tournament that featured "greens" consisting of patterns painted on the desert with drives so long that the cup might not be visible.

The year 1990 saw the arrival of Burning Man, which has blossomed into a weeklong art festival with well over 60,000 attendees. There are many excellent books about Burning Man, so this book focuses on the desert happenings in the period before 1990.

The Black Rock Desert was the site of two successful land speed record attempts in 1983 and 1997; the 1997 effort broke the sound barrier. Amateur rocketry records were set in the Black Rock Desert in 1996 and 2004. The 2004 launch was the first amateur rocket to pass the 100-kilometer limit that defines space flight. A 2007 balloon launch was used as an advertisement for an electronics company. In 2009, Jim Denevan used a Dodge Ram truck to create complex patterns on the desert floor in an area about three miles in diameter. At the time, the work was best viewed from an airplane; today, the work is no longer visible.

In 1999, a group formed the Friends of the Black Rock/High Rock, which helps manage the area and educate the public. This nonprofit organization holds a number of events throughout the year, including an annual rendezvous campout over Memorial Day weekend. The Friends office is located in Gerlach.

In 2000, the Black Rock Desert–High Rock Canyon Emigrant Trails National Conservation Act designated 800,000 acres of the region as a National Conservation Area (NCA) and a partially overlapping 750,000 acres as wilderness. The wilderness areas are closed to wheeled vehicles (except wheelchairs). These restrictions prompted some criticism from longtime visitors, but the NCA will preserve the natural values of the area for future visitors.

The US Gypsum plant closed in 2011, resulting in a dramatic drop in the number of permanent residents. At the time of the closure, the mine at Empire was one of the oldest continuously operating mines west of the Mississippi. In 2013, companies occasionally work the deposits at the mine, which results in a few truckloads being driven to other areas. As of this writing in 2013, Gerlach has a population of roughly 130 people, who support three bars, a gas station, a restaurant, and a general store at Empire. Tourism and cattle ranching are the primary sources of income, though. Recent high gold prices have prompted further activity at the mine near Sulphur, and the area's geothermal energy resources could also provide future permanent jobs.

One

PREHISTORY AND PIONEERS

This chapter begins with the geological history of the area, including a map of Lake Lahontan, images of the Columbian mammoth dig, and images of arrowheads. The latter portion of the chapter follows the Applegate-Lassen Trail and includes locations that pioneers visited as they traveled to California and Oregon. These images are presented in the order that a pioneer or modern visitor would experience them traveling from Rabbit Hole Springs past Black Rock Point and up High Rock Canyon.

The first recorded artist in the area was Joseph Goldsborough Bruff, a topographer who migrated to California in 1849. Bruff's sketch of the carnage at Rabbit Hole Springs brings to life the desperation of pioneers as they realized that Lassen's trail was no easier than the main trail.

In 1854, Lt. Edward G. Beckwith's Pacific Railroad Survey visited the area, and Frederick W. von Egloffstein captured the view from the Selenite Mountains near the future location of Empire, Nevada. The image was published as a four-page panorama in the 1861 survey report.

Daniel Jenks crossed the Smoke Creek Desert in August 1859. He later created a manuscript for his sister from his original notebooks. The manuscript includes 14 crayon drawings, including one of the area. In December 2012, the manuscript sold for $80,000 at auction at Christie's.

This chapter also includes maps by Henry DeGroot (1853) and Israel C. Russell (1883), as well as the art of Craig Sheppard (c. 1970), who also illustrated Sessions S. Wheeler's book *The Black Rock Desert*.

This chapter features photographs taken by Henry Lind in 1941 as he followed the Applegate-Lassen Trail. Lind's documentation offers an early example of automobile-based exploration of the area. Note that quotations from pioneers, artists, photographers, and so forth are reproduced verbatim in the text.

This is the Black Rock that gives its name to the desert and the mountain range. The Black Rock itself is about 300 million years old and consists of volcanic material and fossiliferous limestone. The rock was used as a way marker by pioneers traveling on the Lassen Road or Cutoff to the California gold fields. (University Archives, University of Nevada-Reno, Sessions S. Wheeler Collection 99-06-704.)

This meteorite, discovered in the Black Rock Desert in 2009, is shown as it was found on the playa. Meteorites are typically 4.5 billion years old, which means they are the oldest objects found in the area. However, they must be found within a few decades after they have fallen lest they risk being weathered away or buried. (Jeff Pringle.)

About 12,700 years ago, Lake Lahontan covered the area to depth of about 500 feet. Many of the tufa formations in the area were formed underwater. As the ice age ended, the Lake Lahontan level dropped, leaving "bathtub rings" that are still visible today. Israel C. Russell created this map in 1883. (Mary B. Ansari Map Library, University of Nevada-Reno.)

In 1979, Steve Wallmann discovered a mammoth tooth in the area. In 1981, the site was excavated and the skeletons of several mammoths were exposed. A newspaper reported that the bones were found piled on top of each other, and man-made tools were found nearby, indicating that perhaps the mammoths were hunted. However, a 1991 Desert Research Institute article suggests that the bones were washed down a channel and deposited. (University Archives, University of Nevada-Reno, Sessions S. Wheeler Collection 99-06-71.)

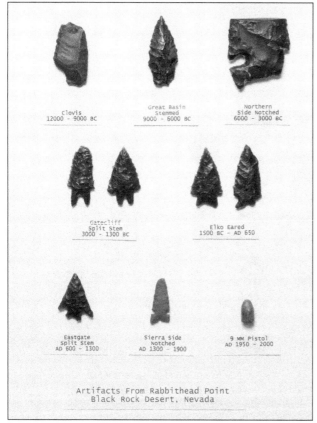

Clovis 12000 - 9000 BC	Great Basin Stemmed 9000 - 6000 BC	Northern Side Notched 6000 - 3000 BC
Gatecliff Split Stem 3000 - 1300 BC		Elko Eared 1500 BC - AD 650
Eastgate Split Stem AD 600 - 1300	Sierra Side Notched AD 1300 - 1900	9 MM Pistol AD 1950 - 2000

Artifacts From Rabbithead Point
Black Rock Desert, Nevada

The excavation process exposed the incomplete tusks of one individual mammoth. The bones were too brittle for display, so museums made molds that were then used to create museum displays. The precise age of the mammoth is unknown, though a nearby site was dated to between 15,000 and 17,000 years old. (University Archives, University of Nevada-Reno, Sessions S. Wheeler Collection 99-06-50.)

Arrowheads are the oldest human-made artifacts found in the area. Archaeologists believe that people have been in the area for at least 11,000 years. The Northern Paiute arrived in the area around 1300 AD and knapped Sierra Side Notched arrowheads. Arrowheads were made from obsidian source material from many locations, including Fox Mountain, located about 60 miles away. (Jeff Pringle.)

In late 1843, John C. Frémont arrived in the region from the north. Frémont traveled through High Rock Canyon and visited Black Rock Springs on January 2, 1844. He went on to visit Trego, ascend Old Razorback, and spend two nights at Great Boiling Springs near present-day Gerlach before departing the area via Pyramid Lake. (Library of Congress.)

A section of Frémont's map shows his 1843–1844 route from the north across Mud Lake to Great Boiling Springs and then south to Pyramid Lake and the Salmon Trout River. Today, Mud Lake is known as the Black Rock Desert, Great Boiling Springs is located just outside of Gerlach, and the Salmon Trout River is known as the Truckee River. (David Rumsey Map Collection, www.davidrumsey.com.)

In 1848, Peter Lassen led 12 wagons through the Black Rock Desert region. Lassen's road left the Humboldt River near the present-day site of the Rye Patch Reservoir, passed through Rabbit Hole Springs and Black Rock Spring, and then continued north through present-day Alturas. Lassen's road was about 200 miles longer than the primary California Trail and led travelers past his ranch. (Department of Special Collections and University Archives, Stanford University Libraries.)

In 1941, Henry Lind traversed the Applegate-Lassen Trail, took photographs, and later wrote on the backs of the images. On the back of this photograph, Lind wrote: "Through a cleft in the Kamma Mountains present-day road nears Rosebud-Rabbit Hole Springs mining district." Lind corresponded with Ruby Swartzlow about the Applegate-Lassen Trail, and Lind's photographs appear in Swartzlow's *Lassen, His Life and Legacy* (1964). (California State University, Chico, Meriam Library Special Collections sc20011; photograph by Henry Lind.)

Lind wrote: "At Rabbit Hole Springs, Nevada. An important spot to emigrants. Water was scarce in pioneer days and scarce now. Dry placering for gold was carried on in the Rabbit Hole district in recent years." In 1860, Col. Frederick W. Lander's group spent two weeks improving the spring and created a six-foot-deep tank that held 80,000 gallons. (California State University, Chico, Meriam Library Special Collections sc20012; photograph by Henry Lind.)

Lind wrote: "Rock Hut built over Rabbit Hole Spring. Used by placer miners as 'cooler' for food supplies." An 1860 letter signed by "Voltigeur" that appears in the *Alta California* newspaper states: "The spring, now ten feet in depth, and walled up with well cemented stone is second to nothing, as far as my limited observation extends, but the artisans of San José." (California State University, Chico, Meriam Library Special Collections sc20013; photograph by Henry Lind.)

In 1849, Joseph Goldsborough Bruff took the Lassen Trail and drew the scene at Rabbit Hole Springs. Bruff wrote: "well hole with hind parts of an ox sticking an out. Dead oxen all around. Air foul." He made a habit of recording graves; at Rabbit Hole Springs, he recorded the grave of a 50-year-old man who had died four days earlier of typhus. (The Huntington Library, San Marino, California.)

In 1854, the area was surveyed by Lt. Edward G. Beckwith's Pacific Railroad Survey expedition as a possible route for the first transcontinental railroad. This view is looking north from what is now known as the Selenite Range east of Empire. The image identifies several locations, including

The University of Nevada Press commissioned Craig Sheppard to create a portfolio called Landmarks of the Emigrant Trail. To prepare the work, Sheppard and Yolande Jacobson traversed the Applegate-Lassen Trail while referring to Joseph Goldsborough Bruff's journal. This painting, titled *Rabbit Hole Springs, 1849*, illustrates a less desperate day than Bruff's sketch on the previous page. The portfolio was published in 1971. (University Archives, University of Nevada-Reno 2004.117.)

"Great Boiling Spring Point," the location of present-day Gerlach, and the Black Rock Range. (David Rumsey Map Collection, www.davidrumsey.com.)

Lind wrote: "Abandoned road west of Rabbit Hole Springs. Probably actual old trail. Present road descends to Sulphur station on W.P.R.R. down canyon to right. Barren flats of Black Rock desert about 30 miles distant." Joseph Goldsborough Bruff describes arriving at the brink of the plateau near Rabbit Hole and finding an acquaintance who was baking bread to feed to his hungry cattle. (California State University, Chico, Meriam Library Special Collections sc20014; photograph by Henry Lind.)

Lind wrote: "Black Rock Point (center) about 15 miles west across desert. Infrequently used road in foreground is likely the old pioneer trail which head west to Black Rock Point in the immediate locality." William White Hobart states that there were so many carcasses here that "by stepping from one body to another one need never to have touched the ground." (California State University, Chico, Meriam Library Special Collections sc20015; photograph by Henry Lind.)

In this June 1959 image, Mark Runnels and Dick Teater retrace the Applegate-Lassen Trail towards the Black Rock Desert. The trail from Rabbit Hole to the Black Rock consists of deep silt that becomes impassible when wet, as well as the Quinn River that must also be crossed. Sessions Wheeler notes that the 1849 diaries do not mention the Quinn, indicating that 1849 was a very dry year. (Nevada Historical Society trails002.)

In 1852, William Nobles developed a trail from the Black Rock Desert through the Smoke Creek Desert and Susanville and then on to Shasta City near present-day Redding. In August 1859, Daniel Jenks travelled this route on his way to Yreka. This drawing is titled *The Dessert* and appears to be either the Black Rock or the nearby Smoke Creek Desert. (Library of Congress.)

During his trip, Lind detoured off the Applegate-Lassen Trail and followed the approximate path of the Nobles Trail southwest to Gerlach. He wrote: "Huge boiling spring at Gerlach, Nevada. At narrows of desert, about 40 miles south of emigrant trail crossing of desert." (California State University, Chico, Meriam Library Special Collections sc20016; photography by Henry Lind.)

Lind wrote: "Smoke Creek Desert, Granite Creek Desert and Black Rock desert make three huge bays in what is called as a whole the Black Rock Desert. This part of the ancient bed of Lake Lahontan stretches over 123 Miles SE to NW in the northwest corner of Nevada. Almost as little known and visited as in the days of pioneer wagon trains." (California State University, Chico, Meriam Library Special Collections sc20017; photograph by Henry Lind.)

Lind wrote: "Jack the Rabbit 'gives up' after a race with the car—far out on the desert floor." Typically, four-legged animals found in the desert during the day had been traversing the desert at night but did not make it all the way across. There are reports of live porcupines and badgers being found in the middle of the playa. (California State University, Chico, Meriam Library Special Collections sc20018; photograph by Henry Lind.)

Lind wrote: "The Big Hot Spring at Black Rock Point. It is said that the parts of wagons, bones of animals have been pulled from the waters. Immigrant camped here after crossing desert. Cooled the waters before using, for man and beast." Joseph Goldsborough Bruff counted 150 dead oxen, two horses, and two mules and noted that his group added three animals to the wolf larder. (California State University, Chico, Meriam Library Special Collections sc20022; photograph by Henry Lind.)

Joseph Goldsborough Bruff describes Black Rock Springs as "a raised circular tumola [tomb?], about 30 feet diameter on top, basin shap'd within, dark bubbling water, overflowing one edge, and received into a circular reservoir, dug some yards lower down and from there into a 3rd reservoir in which it is cool enough to use for ordinary purposes" (The Huntington Library, San Marino, California.)

The Black Rock is in the background of this c. 1987 photograph of a modern sheepherder's wagon. Many northern Nevada sheepherders are Basque, and the Bidarts and Monteros, two Basque families, have operated the Leonard Creek Ranch on the north arm of the Black Rock Desert for many years. In 1966, some 1,200 Basque sheepherders were employed in the United States, but by 1976, there were 106. (Patricia Kelley.)

North of Black Rock Springs are the remains of Hardin City, which include the sites of two silver mills, although very little—if any—silver was produced there. In 1849, J.A. Hardin found silver and lead specimens, but upon his return in 1858, he was unable to find the original source. (University Archives, University of Nevada-Reno, Sessions S. Wheeler Collection 99-06-702.)

Lind wrote: "Back tracking on the Emmigrant trail near Black Rock Point. Forced to turn back at this point by drifting sand." Lind was traveling east on the Lassen Trail from Black Rock Point towards Rabbit Hole, which would have led him across the Quinn River. (California State University, Chico, Meriam Library Special Collections sc20023; photograph by Henry Lind.)

Lind traveled from the Black Rock across the northeast finger of the desert toward the Soldier Meadows road. He wrote: "Black Rock Point, in right center of photo. The desert is dangerous when wet. Even when dry at the surface in June beneath a 3 inch crust was a sticky substance about as soft as modeling clay." (California State University, Chico, Meriam Library Special Collections sc20019; photograph by Henry Lind.)

Lind wrote: "Pahute Mountain in the Black Rock Range. Peter Lassen was killed, murdered, at Clapper Canyon to right in photo." Lassen and Clapper were murdered on April 26, 1859, while prospecting for silver. Clapper was shot while sleeping; Lassen was shot moments later, while standing. Their companion Americus Wyatt rode 140 miles bareback to Susanville to report the murders. (California State University, Chico, Meriam Library Special Collections sc20024; photograph by Henry Lind.)

DeGroot's 1863 map shows the location of Murder Rock and Lassen's grave. The murders remain unsolved; Lassen was on excellent terms with the Paiutes, so the most likely suspect was Americus Wyatt. Lassen's body was later exhumed and moved to Susanville. In 1990, Clapper's remains were found at the murder site. (David Rumsey Map Collection, www.davidrumsey.com.)

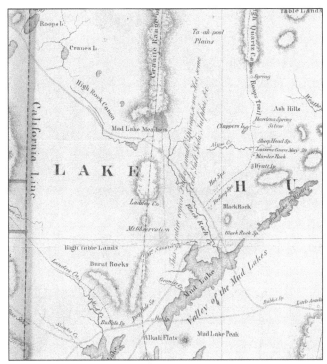

Henry Lind wrote: "Wheeler Ranch. Stock ranch oasis near Black Rock Point." This ranch was established in 1903. Don Wheeler died of exposure in 1922 after his vehicle got stuck crossing the desert. The Parman family purchased Wheeler Ranch in 1927, were forced to sell in the early 1930s, repurchased the ranch in 1937, and operated it until 1958. (California State University, Chico, Meriam Library Special Collections sc20020; photograph by Henry Lind)

Lind wrote: "Ralph Parman runs the Wheeler Ranch pretty much single handed. Was the only person met in backtracking the old Lassen Trail who was both interested and somewhat aware of the historical spots in his country." In 1926, at age 18, Parman was running Soldier Meadows ranch. Parman went on to write three books about the history of the area. (California State University, Chico, Meriam Library Special Collections sc20021; photograph by Henry Lind.)

Lind wrote: "The crossing of Soldier Creek near Mud Springs. June 1941" This image is likely of the area now known as the Mud Meadow Reservoir. This area is probably the "Mud Lake" described by Joseph Goldsborough Bruff in 1849. Near here, Bruff recorded the grave of "C. H. Bintly, from Yorkshire England. Died Sept. 9th. 1849, aged 43 years." (California State University, Chico, Meriam Library Special Collections sc20025; photograph by Henry Lind.)

Lind wrote: "U.S. Cavalry fort at Soldier Meadows ranch, near old emmigrant trail. First used in the 60s (?)" Camp McGarry was located about 10 miles north of Soldier Meadows. Soldier Meadows was used as a winter camp because it is lower in elevation than Camp McGarry. The Army used Camp McGarry from about 1865 until 1868. (California State University, Chico, Meriam Library Special Collections sc20026; photograph by Henry Lind.)

Lind wrote: "Bogged down in the *desert* near Soldier Meadows!" Here, Lind was back on the Lassen Trail at Mud Meadows headed toward Fly Canyon. The pass on the left is Fly Canyon; the pass on the right is the present-day road. (California State University, Chico, Meriam Library Special Collections sc20027; photograph by Henry Lind.)

There are few trees in the Black Rock region, so corrals were sometimes fenced with sagebrush, as shown in this 1920s image. Joseph Goldsborough Bruff describes a similar fence seen while traveling from Mud Meadows to High Rock Canyon: "Indian line over road & hills, for several miles, of sagebrushes inverted & stones, recent seeming." (Nevada Historical Society wa06597.)

Lind wrote: "Looking north—back to Soldier Meadows. Nev. Nearing High Rock Canyon." Joseph Goldsborough Bruff describes this area as "powder & crude rock vol.[canic] mostly. Very rough sharp & bad to animals, vehicles and pedestrians." Continuing his description of the carnage: "six dead oxen, 1 horse and 1 mule." (California State University, Chico, Meriam Library Special Collections sc20028; photograph by Henry Lind.)

Lind wrote: "Entering High Rock region on present-day road." This location is very close to Fly Canyon Wagon Slide, a roughly 200-foot-long, 45-degree slope. Here, pioneers either drove very carefully, lowered their wagons with ropes, put on an extra team to slow the descent, or locked the wheels. (California State University, Chico, Meriam Library Special Collections sc20029; photograph by Henry Lind.)

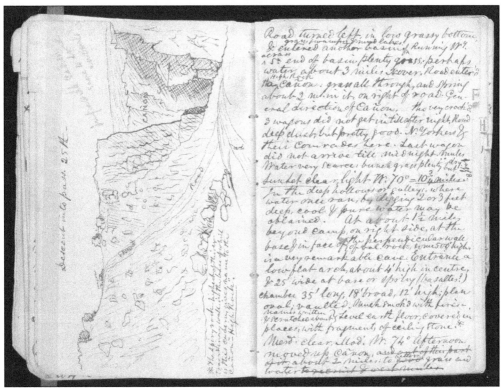

Joseph Goldsborough Bruff drew *Descent into Pass*, which shows wagons descending the Fly Canyon Wagon Slide on September 25, 1849. Bruff wrote, "The declivity and its base, retained vestiges of unfortunate traveling in the shape of broken wagons, wheels, hubs, tires, axels, and 3 dead oxen." (Beinecke Rare Book and Manuscript Library, Yale Collection of Western Americana.)

Lind wrote: "West into Narrows of High Rock Canyon. Emmigrants left names, dates on sheer rock walls. This point cannot be reached by car. June 1941." Today, it is possible to drive to this location in a two-wheel-drive truck. Each year, High Rock Canyon is closed to motorized vehicles in the spring to prevent disturbances to wildlife. (California State University, Chico, Meriam Library Special Collections sc20030; photograph by Henry Lind.)

Lind wrote: "1852 Marking in High Rock Canyon with chisel. 'Cye Cox' in '22 didn't do as good a job." (Fortunately, in 2013, Cye Cox's update is barely visible.) George N. Jaquith was killed in April 1867 during an Army expedition near Steens Mountain in southeastern Oregon. (California State University, Chico, Meriam Library Special Collections sc20032; photograph by Henry Lind.)

Lind wrote: "Looking east in narrows of High Rock Canyon. Emmigrant markings on cliff walls. This point about 2 miles from nearest traversable road." In December 1843, Frémont described the canyon as "a sort of chasm, the little strip of grass under our feet, the rough walls of bare rock on either hand, and the narrow strip of sky above" (California State University, Chico, Meriam Library Special Collections sc20031; photograph by Henry Lind.)

Ruts made by the wagons of pioneers are visible in this hill in High Rock Canyon, pictured here in the 1970s. These days, the road bypasses the ruts, thus preserving them. Iron rust stains are visible at the Fly Canyon Wagon Slide as well. (University Archives, University of Nevada-Reno, Sessions S. Wheeler Collection 99-06-280.)

A caption on the back of this photograph reads: "Henry Lind, in High Rock Canyon. –June 1941." Lind (b. 1900) was fascinated with the west; he described himself as an amateur historian. In his youth, Lind spent summers working in the sign shop at Lassen Volcanic National Park and coauthored a 1929 pamphlet entitled *Lassen Glimpses: the Lassen Park Guide Book*. Lind built a diorama of the Lassen area that was displayed at the Loomis Museum until the late 1960s. Robert Lind, Henry's nephew, reported that rangers would blow cigarette smoke from under the diorama to simulate smoke rising from Mount Lassen. Lind died in 1963 before the appearance of Ruby Swartzlow's Lassen book. Swartzlow specifically thanks Lind in the acknowledgements and notes his then recent passing. Lind's images of Lassen are resold today for between $8 and $20. (California State University, Chico, Meriam Library Special Collections sc20035; photograph by Henry Lind.)

The view looking back to the narrows at the north end of High Rock Canyon is similar to Devil's Gate, Wyoming. Joseph Goldsborough Bruff wrote, "In the narrow canyon, near camp, I noticed the correspondence of the two sides, as I had done in some other volcanic chasms." (University Archives, University of Nevada-Reno, Sessions S. Wheeler Collection 99-06-271.)

To the east of High Rock Lake is Little High Rock Canyon, which is where John Laxague, Peter Erramouspe, Bertrand Indiano, and Harry Cambron were killed in 1911. Mike Daggett's Indian band was accused of the murders. A posse found Daggett's band outside Golconda, and posse member Ed Hogle and eight Indian men, women and children were killed in the shoot-out. (Nevada Historical Society ethnic206.)

This is Mike Daggett's abandoned camp in Little High Rock Canyon. The four men were killed on January 19, 1911, though their bodies were not found until early February. Daggett's group traveled over 200 miles under difficult winter conditions to Kelley Creek, where the posse found them on February 25. (Nevada Historical Society ethnic204.)

This picture of Little High Rock Canyon contains an X marking the location where the bodies were discovered. There is controversy about many of the details of the incident, including about whether the bodies of the four ranchers were disfigured, what happened near Golconda, what tribe Daggett was from, and whether he was known as "Shoshone Mike" before his death. (Nevada Historical Society ethnic205.)

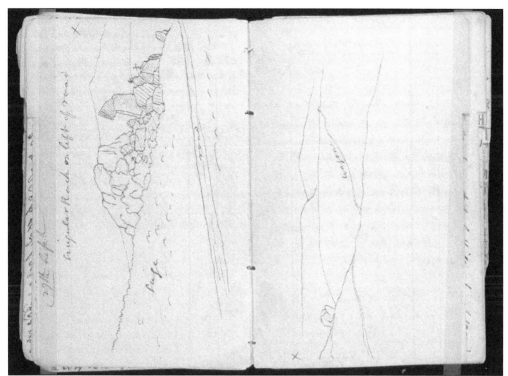

The outcrop shown in Joseph Goldsborough Bruff's *Singular Rock on the Left of the Road* is located near Massacre Ranch, south of Highway 8A. Despite the name, there is no evidence that a massacre ever occurred at Massacre Ranch. The ranch was initially part of the Miller and Lux holdings in the 1920s and was acquired by the Bureau of Land Management. (Beinecke Rare Book and Manuscript Library, Yale Collection of Western Americana)

Joseph Goldsborough Bruff's "Singular Rock" is pictured here in modern times. Trails West is an organization that installs informational markers at sites on emigrant trails. The marker at Bruff's Singular Rock is one of about 600 markers installed and maintained by Trails West. The Oregon-California Trails Association (OCTA) is a similar organization that places markers and helps preserve emigrant trails. (Nevada Historical Society Trail11.)

Lind wrote: "Petrified tree on Gerlach–Cedarville Road." After hiking up High Rock Canyon, Lind drove through little High Rock Canyon back to State Route 34, where he stopped at the petrified forest. Lind saw the petrified forest before he saw Joseph Goldsborough Bruff's Singular Rock. The images of Bruff's rock were placed on the previous page for comparison purposes. (California State University, Chico, Meriam Library Special Collections sc20036; photograph by Henry Lind.)

Lind wrote: "Lassen–Applegate trails passed thru this country. '49 Lake, Nevada." Today this lake is known as Forty-nine Lake and it is a seasonally dry lake located in Long Valley near State Route 34 and Highway 8A. The trail passed across the lakebed when the lake was dry. (California State University, Chico, Meriam Library Special Collections sc20037; photograph by Henry Lind.)

Lind wrote: "Emmigrant carvings in '49 canyon Nevada–east of Cedarville, Cal." The "49" has been repainted so many times that it stands about an inch above the surface of the eroded hot spring cone. This was the site of the Forty Nine House, a way station on the stage road leading from Surprise Valley to Camp McGarry and Denio. (California State University, Chico, Meriam Library Special Collections sc20038; photograph by Henry Lind.)

Lind wrote: "Warner Mountains, Surprise Valley near Cedarville, Cal. Emmigrant trail turned north (right) up Surprise Valley." This photograph was taken near the present-day California-Nevada border looking west to the Warner Mountains. The Warner Mountains were named for Capt. William Horace Warner, who was killed in 1849 just days after Joseph Goldsborough Bruff traveled through the area. (California State University, Chico, Meriam Library Special Collections sc20039; photograph by Henry Lind)

Lind wrote: "Upper Lake in Surprise Valley East from Summit of Fandango Pass, over which emmigrant trail found way." This view looks southward from California toward the Black Rock Desert region. The Hays Canyon Range is visible in the distance at right. (California State University, Chico, Meriam Library Special Collections sc20040; photograph by Henry Lind.)

Two

HOLLYWOOD COMES TO THE BLACK ROCK

In the 1920s, Western-themed movies were big sellers, and filming them on location helped to draw audiences. In 1924, John Ford directed *The Iron Horse*, which was filmed near Wadsworth.

In 1926, the movie *The Winning of Barbara Worth* was filmed in the Black Rock Desert near Trego. The movie was based on Harold Bell Wright's book of the same name, which is loosely based on the accidental flooding of the Salton Sea in Southern California.

In February 1926, director Henry King started a 4,000-mile journey to look for locations for the movie. In April, he and his companions rented a car in Reno and visited Lovelock. They drove through Jungo, then got lost at night, finally arriving at Sulphur to split a meager breakfast of beans amongst five men. Their car overheated near Trego Hot Springs, where a member of the party burned his hands in the hot water. They finally arrived in Gerlach in the late evening, around 10:00 p.m. Despite the hardships of the trip, King decided to film the movie in the Black Rock Desert.

Filming started in earnest in the summer of 1926 and included building the town of Barbara Worth as a set on the Black Rock Desert just north of Trego. The town's mayor was Henry King.

At that time, the filming of *The Winning of Barbara Worth* was the largest recorded artistic endeavor on the Black Rock Desert. The town of Barbara Worth was similar to temporary cities created for other, much larger, artistic events, such as Burning Man, that started in the 1990s.

In 1926, the movie *The Winning of Barbara Worth* was filmed in the Black Rock Desert. Pictured here are director Henry King (third from left) giving Nevada governor James G. Scrugham (center) a tour with stars Vilma Bánky and Ronald Colman at right. The movie was Gary Cooper's first feature role. (Nevada Historical Society ms331-3.)

Nevada governor James G. Scrugham (left) and Ronald Colman are seen on location during the shooting of *The Winning of Barbara Worth*. The movie is based on the book of the same name by Harold Bell Wright. In the movie, an engineer (Colman) is building an irrigation system and competes with a cowboy (Cooper) for the affections of a local girl (Bánky). The story is based on the settling of California's Salton Sink. (Nevada Historical Society ms331-2.)

Gov. James G. Scrugham (left) and director Henry King (right) are pictured here on the movie set. In 1903, Scrugham joined the University of Nevada as an assistant professor of mechanical engineering, and by 1914, he was dean of the college of engineering. As state engineer in the 1920s, he was involved with the planning for the Hoover Dam. He was governor of Nevada from 1923 to 1927. In 1924, he received a package containing Native American artifacts that turned out to be from the Lost City site in the area that was later inundated by the Hoover Dam. Scrugham obtained funding for the excavation of that site. He was elected to the House of Representatives in 1933 and then the Senate in 1942, where he served until his death in 1945. In 1988, historian Phillip I. Earl described Scrugham's visit to the movie set in "Hollywood Comes to the Black Rock: The Story of the Making of *The Winning of Barbara Worth*"; this chapter takes its title from Earl's article. (Nevada Historical Society ms331-1.)

Winnemucca resident Vera Haviland visited the Barbara Worth location and took a series of behind-the-scenes photographs. These are two unidentified extras from the movie. Haviland's shadow is visible in many of the photographs. Here, she is presumably wearing pants and looking down into the top of a view camera. (University Archives, University of Nevada-Reno 3476-151; photograph by Vera Haviland.)

Pictured here is an actor or extra, perhaps from Winnemucca. Vera Haviland's father, Carlton, was the first mayor of Winnemucca. As part of preproduction, producer Samuel Goldwyn contacted Mayor Haviland and the chamber of commerce about office space and possible filming locations in the area. (University Archives, University of Nevada-Reno 3476-150; photograph by Vera Haviland.)

Vera Haviland sits on her bed in a tent. Haviland graduated from the University of Nevada, Reno, in 1926. She married Howard E. Browne, who later served as the district attorney in Lander County for about 15 years. Haviland's grandson Kevin Allec found these photographs in an album and donated them to the University of Nevada, Reno. (University Archives, University of Nevada-Reno 3476-155; photograph by Vera Haviland.)

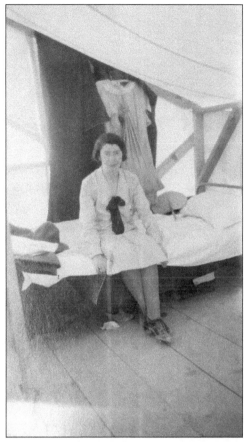

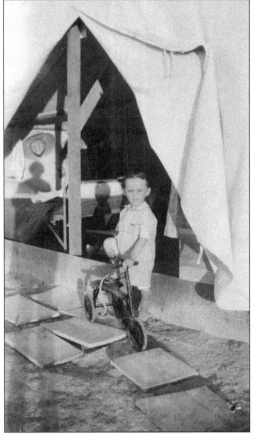

This unidentified young boy stands near a tent as he squints into the sun. During production of *The Winning of Barbara Worth*, there were several minor injuries, including a fall from a porch by Paul Koseris, a Winnemucca boy. That night, Koseris came down with chills, fever, and chest pains. In the evening, Koseris was rushed to Winnemucca via freight train, hospitalized for several days, and recovered within two weeks. (University Archives, University of Nevada-Reno 3476-157; photograph by Vera Haviland.)

This US Mail wagon was used in the movie. The sign says "Rubio City and Kingston," which were two fictitious names created by Harold Bell Wright. For the filming, three sets were constructed, one just north of Trego (named Barbara Worth), one in Gerlach, and one at the sand dunes near Blue Mountain, west of Winnemucca. (University Archives, University of Nevada-Reno 3476-156; photograph by Vera Haviland.)

The view in this image looks northwest from near Barbara Worth toward a tent and a wagon train with the Calico Mountains in the background. Mayor Carlton Haviland also ran a stage line, and some of his horses were used in the movie. Horses, livestock, and wagons used in filming came from as far away as Battle Mountain. (University Archives, University of Nevada-Reno 3476-172; photograph by Vera Haviland.)

In this image, possibly the same three wagons shown in the previous image are fully loaded and heading south with the Granite Range in the background. Vilma Bánky wrote that the horseback riding on the Black Rock Desert was wonderful and that most evenings, riding parties could be seen taking advantage of the smooth surface. (University Archives, University of Nevada-Reno 3476-166; photograph by Vera Haviland.)

The writing on this wagon refers to the fictional town of Barba. The June 10, 1926, *Humboldt Star* newspaper carries a notice that Lovelock rancher W.H. Cooper is seeking farm animals and wagons in poor condition for use in the movie; Cooper obtained 50 horses, 25 fresno scrapers, 20 wagons, and 100 tons of hay. (University Archives, University of Nevada-Reno 3476-154; photograph by Vera Haviland.)

Here, Gary Cooper looks at bones that were possibly used in the beginning of the movie. *The Winning of Barbara Worth* was Cooper's first feature role, for which he was paid $50 per week. Paramount, a competitor of Samuel Goldwyn's, signed Cooper to a long-term contract after *Barbara Worth*. (University Archives, University of Nevada-Reno 3476-160; photograph by Vera Haviland.)

Pictured here is Paul McAllister, who plays the part of Henry Lee, "The Seer," in the movie. The Seer has the initial vision to bring water to the desert and is present when the infant Barba was found and later adopted by Mr. Worth. In the movie, Henry is the father of Gary Cooper's character, Abe Lee. (University Archives, University of Nevada-Reno 3476-158; photograph by Vera Haviland.)

This is the diminutive Clyde Cook, who plays a comedic role in *The Winning of Barbara Worth*. Born in Australia, Cook was first known as "The Kangaroo Boy" because of his contortionist abilities. Later in life, he was known as the "Rubber Comedian." In an early scene in the movie, Cook is literally tied in knots during a fight. (University Archives, University of Nevada-Reno 3476-149; photograph by Vera Haviland.)

In the movie, a weakness in a dam is identified and some of the residents of Kingston move to the new town of Barba. These two unidentified men appeared in a celebration scene in Barba. Some of the cowboys who were hired as extras played musical instruments and taught guitar to some of the actors. (University Archives, University of Nevada-Reno 3476-161; photograph by Vera Haviland.)

Here, Vilma Bánky is writing while seated on the porch. The movie includes a very similar scene with Bánky writing and wearing the same dress. Bánky wrote to *Los Angeles Times* columnist Grace Kinsley and stated that because most thermometers stop at 120 degrees, the residents of Barbara Worth did not know how warm it was between noon and 3:00. (University Archives, University of Nevada-Reno 3476-163; photograph by Vera Haviland.)

Here, Vilma Bánky is receiving a message via horseback. Bánky and Ronald Colman were both under contract with United Artists, and neither was enthusiastic about coming to the desert. Bánky had just finished making *Son of the Sheik* with Rudolph Valentino, which turned out to be his last film. Colman's previous film was *Beau Geste*. (University Archives, University of Nevada-Reno 3476-175; photograph by Vera Haviland.)

Vilma Bánky stands on the porch of a set. In the evenings, Bánky reportedly spent her free time listening to the radio. The set had a newspaper, the *Barbara Worth Times*, which reports that Bánky had made a pet out of a desert chipmunk. Bánky also wrote that during Gov. James Scrugman's visit, a colt was born and named Barbara. (University Archives, University of Nevada-Reno 3476-159; photograph by Vera Haviland.)

The people shown here are unidentified but are possibly actors or extras from *The Winning of Barbara Worth*, though there were many visitors to the location. The movie was made during Prohibition, but the rumor was that cast members had their own private stocks of alcohol. The site was just inside Pershing County, so three deputy sheriffs were stationed there; United Artists paid $4.50 of their $5 per day salary. (University Archives, University of Nevada-Reno 3476-164; photograph by Vera Haviland.)

This Ford Model T and its occupants appear in *The Winning of Barbara Worth*—the automobile gets stuck in the sand, and then the man says, "Wind her up again, Ma." (University Archives, University of Nevada-Reno 3476-165; photograph by Vera Haviland.)

It was reported that over 2,000 human residents of Nevada were employed during the filming, the bulk of which occurred over two months. Extras from Reno were paid $3 per day. The production company covered their food, lodging, and travel to and from the set. (University Archives, University of Nevada-Reno 3476-167; photograph by Vera Haviland.)

This mule train in *The Winning of Barbara Worth* is probably used in the film to depict settlers fleeing the flooding. Human activity on the lakebed stirs up dust, which is a constant irritation. The east side, where filming occurred, is typically dustier than the upwind west side. (University Archives, University of Nevada-Reno 3476-168; photograph by Vera Haviland.)

During the filming of *Barbara Worth*, temperatures ranged as high as 105 Fahrenheit (and 124 Fahrenheit in the commissary tent). To avoid the heat of the day, director Henry King started filming at 5:00 a.m. by sounding the sirens at the dining hall. Filming ended at 6:00 p.m., followed by showers, dinner, movies, and music. (University Archives, University of Nevada-Reno 3476-169; photograph by Vera Haviland.)

The town of Barbara Worth consisted of many false-front buildings. During the second day of filming, a sandstorm blew down many of the sets and tents. A cloudburst then made the road to Gerlach impassable. Production was delayed three days for repairs. After filming was completed, Lewis King sold the building materials to the Gerlach Land and Livestock Company. (University Archives, University of Nevada-Reno 3476-170; photograph by Vera Haviland.)

This photograph shows a crew filming a scene for *The Winning of Barbara Worth*. Exposed film was transported by train and then airplane to Goldwyn's headquarters at the DeMille studios in Los Angeles. The *Los Angeles Times* reported that this movie was the first time that cast and crew members of a film company were transported to and from location via an airmail plane. (University Archives, University of Nevada-Reno 3476-175; photograph by Vera Haviland.)

Livestock were kept in yards near Trego Hot Springs. For production purposes, special trains were run from Winnemucca to Trego. This view looks west toward the Granite Range. It is possible that a scene is being filmed at left—a reflector is visible. (University Archives, University of Nevada-Reno 3476-171; photograph by Vera Haviland.)

This wagon is being led by mules and a white horse. Although they were slower than horses, mules were preferred by pioneers because they required less grain and were more sure-footed. Oxen were slower than mules, but were preferred over mules because they could be sold for more money in California. (University Archives, University of Nevada-Reno 3476-173; photograph by Vera Haviland.)

The filming required many wagons, horses, and mules. The *Los Angeles Times* reported that during the filming of a scene, Tom Loy's team of broncos unexpectedly bolted. Loy dropped one rein and pulled harder on the other, which caused the team to turn in tight circles as pots and pans flew out of the wagon. (University Archives, University of Nevada-Reno 3476-174; photograph by Vera Haviland.)

Three

Ranches, Mines, and Towns

After the pioneers, the story of the Black Rock Desert continued with the arrival of ranchers and miners. In 1856, Ladue Vary established the ranch at Deep Hole Springs, which is located at the north end of the Smoke Creek Desert, about nine miles east of present-day Gerlach. Several murders and cattle thefts at Deep Hole are chronicled by Fairfield in his *History of Lassen County.*

Deep Hole was eventually purchased by Louis Gerlach, a rancher from Stockton who went on to purchase other Black Rock area ranches and form the Gerlach Land and Livestock Company. The town of Gerlach was named after Louis Gerlach when the Western Pacific Railway came through in 1905 and 1906. Louis' son Fred owned the Fly Ranch for many years. After Louis's death in 1921, the company was sold to Ed Waltz and became the Gerlach and Waltz Company.

Louis Gerlach hired James Raser to manage the ranches. Raser developed a mine at Donnelly Mountain and is said to have discovered gypsum between 1910 and 1916 at what would become the town of Empire. In 1922, Pacific Portland Cement began operations in the area and soon moved its operations from a previous location, also known as Empire, located near Carson City. The property was purchased by US Gypsum in 1948 and operated until 2011.

The construction of the Western Pacific Railroad meant that Gerlach was now a crew-change and water stop. At one time, Gerlach had a railroad roundhouse and two water towers, one of which was still standing as of 2013.

An unidentified ranch hand (left), Fred Gerlach (center), and Jigger Bob are pictured with a butchered hog around 1910. Bob worked for the Pyramid Lake Police and earned $20 per month in 1915. He was reported to have been 114 years old when he died, though census data indicates he was in his 90s. (Nevada Historical Society WA490.)

This 1910 image shows James Raser and his pet deer. Raser was Louis Gerlach's ranch foreman for many years. In 1905, a tick at Deep Hole Ranch bit Gerlach. Due to fears of tick fever, Gerlach rushed to Reno, where the tick was found to be a type that did not carry fever. Gerlach is said to never have returned to Deep Hole. (Nevada Historical Society wa00497.)

This 1910 image shows James Raser at the Petrified Forest. Raser ran Louis Gerlach's operation like it was his own; Raser was listed as the postmaster of Deep Hole in 1894. In 1920, Raser's leg was broken while branding cattle, which caused him to use a cane and ride a buckboard. Raser was fired after Gerlach's death in 1921. (Nevada Historical Society wa06252.)

A Mr. and Mrs. Whitaker are pictured at Deep Hole sometime between 1890 and 1910. Deep Hole was an important ranch in the area for many years and had the only area store in the early 1900s. Frederick W. Lander negotiated an informal cease-fire with Numaga at Deep Hole in 1861, though there were murders at Deep Hole in 1862 and 1869. (University Archives, University of Nevada-Reno 07-01-03.)

COWBOYS AT DEEP HOLE

This c. 1900 photograph shows cowboys at Deep Hole. In the 1890s, Louis Gerlach bought the Deep Hole, Clear Creek, and Granite Creek ranches. He eventually owned eight ranches spread over about 60 miles. James Raser hired men like Ed Tonkin and Abe Addington to manage each ranch. (University Archives, University of Nevada-Reno 07-01-12.)

In 1883, Israel Cook Russell wrote that Buffalo Salt Works, near the "Smokey Creek Desert," produced 250 tons of salt annually and that a total of 1,500 tons had been produced to date. Brine was pumped into vats, where the water evaporated and "the crust of salt that remains is then gathered and is found sufficiently pure for household use." (University Archives, University of Nevada-Reno 07-01-18.)

The gravel pit at Sand Pass provided material for the Western Pacific Railroad's 1934 grade renewal project. In this image from between 1930 and 1950, two railroad buildings, still standing as of 2012, are visible in the middle distance. Sand Pass is located at the southern end of the Smoke Creek Desert. (University Archives, University of Nevada-Reno, Jay A. Carpenter Collection 88-55-1089.)

James Raser managed the Donnelly Mountain Mine, located 40 miles west of Gerlach and 10 miles north of Leadville. There are conflicting accounts as to whether a cowboy discovered gold and sold the claim to Raser or if Raser discovered it himself. This c. 1890–1910 photograph is labeled "Donnley Mt Camp," which is a misspelling of Donnelly. (University Archives, University of Nevada-Reno 07-01-09.)

GOING TO DONNELY MT.

This c. 1890–1910 photograph is labeled "Going to Donnely Mt." and is a rare early photograph of the region in winter. The 1913 annual report of the State Inspector of Mines reported that deep winter snow meant that ore could only be taken out in the summer. (University Archives, University of Nevada-Reno 07-01-10.)

This 1910 image shows Donnelly Mine. The 1913 report states, "today he has an up-to-date 5-stamp mill, plates and concentrator. The mill is run by a 35-horsepower Charter gasoline engine. The mine is developed through a series of tunnels to a depth of 250 feet. The vein is very flat and the stopes are held by stulls and back filling." (Nevada Historical Society wa06354.)

This 1912 image shows the Craven Copper Company headframe, located in the Red Butte Mining District, 15 miles north of Sulphur. By the 1930s, the district had produced a small quantity of copper ore, lead-zinc-silver ore, and antimony ore. Most of the production occurred during World War I. (Humboldt Museum, Winnemucca.)

Before 1909, freight team wagons were used to move ore from Sulphur, Nevada. In 1869, a Paiute discovered a deposit of sulfur on the eastern edge of the Black Rock Desert just north of Rabbit Hole. The Paiute sold his claim for a horse and saddle, which he never received. By 1900, men had begun mining the deposit, and the town adopted the name Sulphur. (Nevada Historical Society hu00419.)

Mules were a common form of transportation in the region. Ore was transported by mule in 100- to 110-pound sacks. This cart appears to be of the same vintage as the carts photographed during the 1926 filming of *The Winning of Barbara Worth*. The 1910 Nevada mining report stated that "about 150 tons per month are produced. Twenty-five men are employed. About one-half of them are foreigners." (Humboldt Museum, Winnemucca.)

In the fall of 1909, the Western Pacific Railroad drilled a 970-foot oil well at Sulphur. A heavy grease was reported at three depths, but analysis indicated that the grease was "similar to a product used for lubricating slow moving machinery" and was likely introduced into the well. (Humboldt Museum, Winnemucca.)

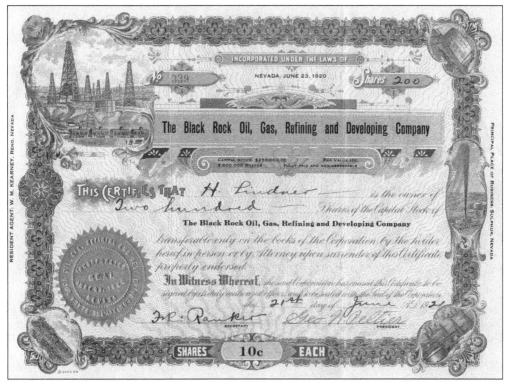

Stock in the Black Rock Oil, Gas, Refining and Developing Company sold for 10¢ per share in June 1921. The company drilled an 800-foot well at Sulphur, but no oil was found. In 1975, the *Humboldt Star* reported that the Bureau of Land Management was taking applications for oil and gas leases. In 1983, a 7,931-foot well drilled near King Lear showed traces of oil. (Nevada Historical Society ms-blackrockoil-01.)

In the 1920s, the Sulphur Hotel was available for visitors who were shipping and receiving via rail. Cattle were driven from surrounding ranches, such as Soldier Meadows, to Sulphur for shipment to California. In 1920, the population of Sulphur was 62, and it dropped to 42 in 1930. (Nevada Historical Society hu00661.)

George W. Swager was the postmaster of the Sulphur post office in 1933. A 1926 accident report from Sulphur describes the death of 19-year-old Mark A. Stritch, who "opened the clamps holding the head of the retort before allowing the release of the pressure of the retort . . . he was blown a distance of 100 feet and when found was dead." (Humboldt Museum, Winnemucca.)

In the 1930s, the Sulphur railway station provided the easiest access to town. In the 1950s, Sulphur boasted a post office, gas station, grocery store, and bar contained in a single building. A nearby grass airstrip appears on current maps. The sulfur mine closed in 1954, though as of 2013, a nearby gold mine is still in operation. (Humboldt Museum, Winnemucca.)

Joe T. Camp edited and published the *Gerlach Express* newspaper in June and July 1914. The advertisers include three saloons, all of which carried the choicest liquors, wines, and cigars. Gerlach has had as many as six bars, which is impressive for an area that even today is almost 80 miles from the nearest stoplight in Fernley. The lead article in this issue calls for "The Re-establishment of Old Roop County," which would have included Gerlach. Roop County was originally named Lake County and then renamed after Isaac Roop, the second governor of Nataqua Territory. (Lassen was the first governor.) Nataqua County was an unofficial territory that was created by its residents to avoid paying taxes in Plumas County, California. Roop County existed from 1862 until 1864, when a survey put most of the county in California. (Nevada Historical Society.)

In the 1920s, the Gerlach Railroad Depot was a two-story building. At some point, the building was replaced with the current structure. Gerlach is halfway between Winnemucca and Portola, so Gerlach was a crew change station. Gerlach had a roundhouse that burned down in 1914 but was later rebuilt. (Nevada Historical Society wa06250.)

Ice crystals cover trees and fences in the 1920s at the Gerlach Store during a day of pogonip. Pogonip is a type of ice fog that occurs when the humidity is near 100 percent and the temperature is well below 32 degrees. In 1887, the *American Meteorological Journal* reported: "To breathe the pogonip is death to the lungs." Happily, this is not true. (Nevada Historical Society wa06251.)

The Gerlach Hotel and Western Pacific water tower are pictured here during a day of pogonip in the 1920s. The water tower holds 40,000 gallons and was constructed in 1909. There are newspaper articles that state that the tower fell down in a 1932 earthquake, but later articles state that the water tower did not actually fall down. (Nevada Historical Society wa06254.)

Beverly Osborn (née Phillips) came to Gerlach in 1947 and returned in the 1960s with her husband, Arley. They bought the Miner's Club bar in 1969, which was the year that her son, James McKnight, was killed in Vietnam. Now in her 80s, Osborn continues to operate the bar each night as of this writing in March 2013. (Beverly Osborn.)

Standing in front of Beverly Osborn's Gerlach home in the winter during the 1940s are Stella Nash (left), Beverly Osborn (center) and Mary Jane Phillip. Nash was visiting from Tucson. In 2013, Osborn still owned the home on the corner of Main Street and Del Ora Avenue. (Beverly Osborn.)

Wesley and Theodosia Fick owned Soldier Meadows between 1947 and 1959. Nell Murbarger interviewed them in 1956 and wrote that their ranch home was constructed to take into account the original buildings constructed in the 1860s. Wesley Fick and Vern and Ralph Parmans were involved in a 1955 lawsuit concerning 150 of the Parmans' cattle. The Parmans won damages of $2,827.20. (University Archives, University of Nevada-Reno 85-08-32541; photograph by Gus Bundy.)

This May 1946 photograph of the Petrified Forest states that the stump is 56 inches in diameter and 84 inches high. The photograph is from the collection of Jay A. Carpenter, who was a professor of mining at University of Nevada, Reno from 1926 until 1951. Many of the following photographs are probably from university field trips. (University Archives, University of Nevada-Reno, Jay A. Carpenter Collection 88-55-1096.)

Around 1910, James Raser discovered gypsum south of Gerlach. The reports and notices section of the *1911 Nevada State Mining Report* notes, "Empire Gypsum Pit, Empire District: That in portions of the pit, which were pointed out to you, the ground is left too perpendicular." This 1928 image shows a cave in the quarry face. (University Archives, University of Nevada-Reno, Jay A. Carpenter Collection 88-55-0463.)

A 1928 close up of the cave in the previous image illustrates the scale of the cave. In 1922, the Pacific Portland Cement Company started construction of a mill at the present-day site of the town of Empire. At the time of the mine's closure in 2011, it was one of the oldest continuously operating mines in the west. (University Archives, University of Nevada-Reno, Jay A. Carpenter Collection 88-55-0465.)

The gypsum mine is shown with the Selenite Range in the background. At left is a white pile of screened gypsum ready to be transported to the mill at Empire. One of the tramline towers is visible in front of the pile of gypsum. (University Archives, University of Nevada-Reno, Jay A. Carpenter Collection 88-55-0936; photograph by Otis A. Kittle.)

This photograph from May 17, 1946, shows a churn drill on the horizon at the Pacific Portland Company Gypsum Quarry. Churn drills use a reciprocating motion to raise and drop the drill bit. The bottom of the 108-foot hole was in eight feet of anhydrite, which, with the addition of water, is transformed into gypsum. (University Archives, University of Nevada-Reno, Jay A. Carpenter Collection 88-55-0382.)

Pacific Portland Cement Company built the Empire community hall in 1924. The community hall also served as a schoolhouse during the time after the old schoolhouse burned down but before the new schoolhouse was built. After the construction of the new community center, this building was torn down in 1985. (University Archives, University of Nevada-Reno, James R. Herz Collection 92-01-5993.)

This May 18, 1946, image shows the gypsum plant in front of the trees of Empire. The Fox Range is visible in the distance. The elevated structure on the left is the lower terminal house of the tramway used to carry gypsum to the mill. The tramway was 5.2 miles long and consisted of 57 towers. (University Archives, University of Nevada-Reno, Jay A. Carpenter Collection 88-55-1101.)

This July 1951 image shows the tramline that was used to transport gypsum from the quarry to the plant. The tramline, originally used at the New Empire mine near Carson City, was moved to the Empire location in 1923. The tramline operated until December 1954. (University Archives, University of Nevada-Reno 85-08-30466; photograph by Gus Bundy.)

The US Gypsum plant is shown in the foreground, with Gerlach to the right with the Granite Range in the background. The tramline towers are visible at right, with State Route 34 (now known as Highway 447) in the foreground. In 1973, the history of the tramway was documented by students at Gerlach High School and reproduced in the *Nevada Historical Society Quarterly*. The tramway towers were built with Chinese labor. Each shift consisted of one mechanic, four operators, and a tram rider. The tram rider would ride the buckets from tower to tower and lubricate the pulleys. This job was fairly dangerous; one tram rider was killed after falling 450 feet from one of the highest towers. The difference in elevation between the highest tower and the mill was 1,300 feet, so the tramway used electric motors as brakes. During a power failure, there was a risk of a runaway. To stop the runaway, brakes had to be applied at the bull wheels at each terminal. (University Archives, University of Nevada-Reno, James R. Herz Collection 92-01-5956.)

These students are vising the Pacific Portland Cement gypsum quarry (also known as the Empire gypsum quarry) on July 2, 1941. They were traveling as part of an S. Frank Hunt Foundation trip. Hunt made his fortune developing a copper mine near Mountain City, north of Elko, Nevada. Hunt, who did not hold a college degree, felt that success was determined by combining scientific understanding with fieldwork. Hunt donated stock, funds, and exploration equipment to create

a foundation at the University of Nevada, Reno, to support field trips in the Great Basin. This image illustrates that industry can be artistic; the whiteness of the gypsum almost overwhelms the camera while darkening the faces of the students. (University Archives, University of Nevada-Reno, Jay A. Carpenter Collection 88-55-0533.)

In 1974, this General Electric 70-ton switcher diesel locomotive (No. 101) was used by US Gypsum to move railcars the six miles between the plant at Empire and the main line at Gerlach. In the 1980s, the locomotive was sometimes operated by an all-female crew. (E.O. Gibson, Wx4.org.)

This chapter closes with a beautiful image of the 1969 Gerlach Garage. That year, regular gasoline was 38.9¢ per gallon, and special was 40.9¢. The 1969 nationwide average price for regular gas was 35¢; the difference represents the cost of serving a small market 75 miles from the interstate. (Nevada Historical Society wa00913.)

Four

THE AUTOMOBILE COMES TO THE BLACK ROCK

After World War II, automobile tourism became more common in the Black Rock Desert. Nevada State Route 34 (now known as State Route 447) from Nixon to Gerlach was not completely paved until the late 1950s or early 1960s. However, that did not stop intrepid visitors from exploring the region.

In the 1950s, Nell Murbarger started writing about her visits to the area. Murbarger wrote a number of articles about the area for *Desert Magazine*, including pieces about the Petrified Forest, Hardin City, Josie Pearl, and the Black Rock Desert Gunnery Range.

The story of the Gunnery Range is complex and somewhat mysterious. As of 2013, shell casings can still be found in the desert, yet since this was an aerial gunnery range, there was almost no other evidence on the ground. In 1945, the North Lovelock Range consisted of about 700,000 acres. In 1949, the name was changed to the Black Rock Desert Gunnery Range, and the size was reduced to 272,000 acres. In 1955, a request was made to increase the range to 1,372,160 acres, though the request was denied due to public opposition. The range closed in 1964.

In 1956, the playwright Arthur Miller was staying at a Pyramid Lake ranch to gain residency so that he could get a divorce in order to free himself up to marry Marilyn Monroe. During his stay, he saw a number of local events, including the roundup of wild horses that would be sold for pet food. Miller wandered the area and almost certainly visited Gerlach. In his autobiography, *Timebends: A Life*, Miller describes traveling with two cowboy horse hunters and visiting a town where the men from the nearby wallboard plant drank heavily in bars.

Miller's story eventually became a movie called *The Misfits*, which turned out to be the last movie for both Marilyn Monroe and Clark Gable. *The Misfits* was not filmed in the Black Rock Desert but instead near Dayton, Nevada, and Pyramid Lake in 1960.

This chapter includes photographs of a horse roundup taken in 1951 by Gus Bundy. These strongly emotional images are part of the story of artistic endeavors in the area.

Josie Pearl (pictured) was a prospector who lived in the Black Rock Range. Ernie Pyle wrote three pages about her in *Home Country*, in which he described her as wearing mismatched men's shoes, yet having $6,000 of diamonds on her wrist. Pyle, a World War II correspondent, wrote to Pearl 13 hours before his death in 1945. In that letter, Pyle wrote that he would never be happier than when he was sitting at her table and eating her Boston baked beans. (A sniper killed Pyle later that day.) Pearl was born in Evening Shade, Arkansas. Her family moved to Creede, Colorado, where she met and married Lane Pearl, a Stanford graduate and mining engineer. Lane died of influenza in 1918, and in the 1920s, Josie settled near Leonard Creek in the Black Rock Range, where she worked claims and grubstaked other prospectors. (Nell Murbarger, Nevada Historical Society, BIO-P-226.)

Gus Bundy captured this photograph of Josie Pearl in August 1955, when she was 79. Pearl operated the Juanita mine for many years, first on her own and later with assistance. During her time at the Juanita, she had to fend off high-graders and con artists. (University Archives, University of Nevada-Reno 85-08-13169; photograph by Gus Bundy.)

With the coming of the atomic age, there was much interest in uranium prospecting. This August 1955 photograph shows a man using a Geiger counter near the Josie Pearl Mine. There is no record of a uranium mine in the Black Rock area, though Gerlach did start removing uranium from the water in the 2000s. (University Archives, University of Nevada-Reno 85-08-13180; photograph by Gus Bundy.)

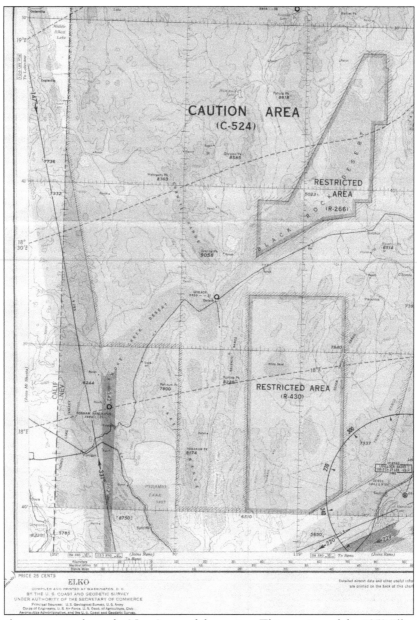

Nell Murbarger wrote about the Navy's use of the region. This portion of the 1959 Elko Section Aeronautical Chart shows the Black Rock Desert Restricted Area (R-266), used for "Air-to-Air Gunnery, Rocket, Bombing and Photograph Flash Bombs" and the Sahwave Mountains Restricted Area (R-266) used for "Air-to-Air Gunnery." Flight was prohibited at altitudes of 60,000 feet and below in the Black Rock Desert area from one hour before sunrise until one hour after sunset. Flight at 15,000 feet was further prohibited from one hour after sunset until 1:00 a.m. There were no flight restrictions on Sundays. Flight in the Sahwave area was restricted at all times and at all altitudes. In addition, most of the surrounding area was in the Fallon No. 1 (C-524) Caution Area, which was used for extensive training from 8:00 a.m. until midnight. The reverse side of this map states, "Flight within Caution Area is not restricted, but pilots are advised to exercise extreme caution." (Special Collections, University of Nevada, Las Vegas Library.)

Herds of wild horses and burros are found throughout the west and around the Black Rock Desert. Although they were descended from domestic horses, these horses were considered feral—meaning that they did not belong to anyone. In the 1950s, some of these animals were rounded up and sent to slaughterhouses to make pet food. Velma Bronn Johnston, also known as "Wild Horse Annie," became interested in their plight and was responsible for a series of laws being passed that addressed how these animals were treated. In September 1951, Edward Gourley and Gus Bundy were taking pictures during a wild horse roundup. Gourley's camera was confiscated, but Bundy's was not. This photograph by Bundy on a playa south of Gerlach shows a herd of wild horses. Bundy's photographs made the world aware of the cruel treatment of wild horses and were used in the campaign to address the issue through laws and regulations. (University Archives, University of Nevada-Reno 85-08-32617; photograph by Gus Bundy.)

These are the tools used in a 1951 roundup with Bill Garaventa. Initially, a light airplane was used to spot the animals and herd them onto a playa. In 1954, A.J. Leibling wrote "The Mustang Buzzers" for the *New Yorker*. In his article, he describes the activities of Garaventa (a pilot) and Hugh Marchbanks (a cowboy). (University Archives, University of Nevada-Reno 85-08-32626; photograph by Gus Bundy.)

After spotting the horses and herding them onto a playa, the next step was to lasso the animals from a truck. Today, the Bureau of Land Management maintains the number of animals by periodically gathering horses using helicopters. The animals are then made available for adoption or placed in long-term care. The BLM does not transfer animals to slaughter. (University Archives, University of Nevada-Reno 85-08-32700; photograph by Gus Bundy.)

During 1950s roundups, after the horse had been lassoed, the next step was to have the animal drag a tire until it was exhausted. In the 1950s, Arthur Miller wrote *The Misfits*, which was about cowboys in the horse roundup trade. In 1961, *The Misfits* was made into a film that stars Marilyn Monroe, Clark Gable, Montgomery Clift, and Eli Wallach. (University Archives, University of Nevada-Reno 85-08-32699; photograph by Gus Bundy.)

After the horse became exhausted, it was then lassoed and brought down for hobbling. There is conjecture that Miller's characters Gay Langland (Clark Gable) and Guido (Eli Wallach) are based on Bill Garaventa and Hugh Marchbanks. There are scenes in the film version of *The Misfits* that strongly resemble Gus Bundy's images. (University Archives, University of Nevada-Reno 85-08-32630; photograph by Gus Bundy.)

The last stage in the roundup involved hobbling the horse and then putting it into a trailer or truck. As late as 1967, wild horse roundups were seen as possible advertising opportunities. There is record of a photograph shoot of a "Wild Horse Hunt" for the *Ford Truck Times*, though the article never appeared. (University Archives, University of Nevada-Reno 85-08-32627; photograph by Gus Bundy.)

This c. 1950s photograph is labeled "Seven wild horses running on the Black Rock Desert," though the location is likely Kumiva Valley, south of Trego, or the Smoke Creek Desert. The Bureau of Land Management stated that in 2012, there were 19,881 wild horses and burros in Nevada, though "appropriate management level" was 12,778 horses and burros. (University Archives, University of Nevada-Reno 85-08-41424; photograph by Gus Bundy.)

Five

NEW ART FORMS FOR AN OLD LANDFORM

In the 1960s and 1970s the Black Rock Desert region started to become a travel destination for both work and pleasure.

In the 1960s, the US Air Force became interested in using dry lakebeds as emergency landing strips for cargo aircraft and the X-15 rocket plane. Geologists who were funded to research the dry lakebeds came to the region and sometimes brought their families.

The 1960s and 1970s brought artists to the region. Among them was Michael Heizer, who created land art on the playa in 1968. Land art is a form of art where the landscape and the art are tightly coupled. Land art typically uses natural material; in this case, Heizer dug trenches in the playa that were then lined with wood.

In July 1969, Walter De Maria filmed *Hard Core*, which features him and Heizer. *Hard Core* was commissioned by a public TV station in San Francisco as part of an eight-artist project. *Hard Core* was described as half-hour long shoot-out scene from a Western. The work consists primarily of several long circular pans with a shoot-out toward the end. De Maria went on to create many pieces—his best known piece is the *Lightning Field*, which consists of 200 stainless-steel poles located in New Mexico.

In the 1970s, John Bogard moved to the area and set up his ceramics studio. Bogard was instrumental in producing a number of events over the years, including an inner-tube rodeo featured in this chapter.

In 1972, National Geographic filmed the television documentary *The Haunted West* in Gerlach; the program features the residents of Gerlach purchasing the town from the Western Pacific Railroad and includes a segment in which the female-operated volunteer fire truck puts out a fire.

In the late 1970s, photographers such as Patricia Kelley visited the area and recorded their impressions.

This chapter is in roughly chronological order and focuses on the artistic efforts in the area. Heizer's work and the inner-tube rodeo both required large flat areas that are really only found in dry lakebeds such as the Black Rock Desert.

This unidentified man is examining incidental dunes near the 12-mile entrance to the Black Rock Desert. During the 1960s, the US Air Force became interested in the dry lakebeds as places to land aircraft such as the X-15. Geologists like James Neal researched processes that affect the surface. Similar dunes have become more common since the year 2000. (James T. Neal.)

In 1969, Wallace R. Hansen of the US Geological Survey took this picture of Old Razorback Mountain from the Selenite Mountains with the Black Rock Desert in the background. Old Razorback Mountain is this formation's formal name, but the mountain is also known as Mount Trego, Trego Peak, and Sleeping Elephant. (Wallace R. Hansen, USGS.)

In 1968, Michael Heizer created nine land art installations in California and Nevada dry lakebeds; the piece was named *Nine Nevada Depressions*. Number eight, titled *Dissipate*, was created on the Black Rock Desert about a mile from the 12-mile entrance. *Dissipate* consisted of six tapered wooden boxes about twelve feet long and one foot square. Heizer determined the orientation of the five trenches by dropping five matchsticks onto a piece of paper and then gluing them where they lay. None of the original nine pieces survive, though some of the pieces, including *Dissipate*, were reproduced by Heizer and now are part of the Menil Collection in Houston. In 1969, Heizer went on to create *Double Negative*, located in Lincoln County. This piece consists of a 1,500-foot trench dug across a canyon. Heizer's 2012 piece *Levitated Mass* is a 340-ton boulder located at the Los Angeles Museum of Art. (Yale Joel/Life Magazine/Getty Images.)

This beautiful April 1973 photograph of the Gerlach Hot Springs is an excellent example of the artistic photography coming out of the Black Rock Desert area. The photograph looks northeast with Old Razorback in the center and the Selenite Range at right. The 1960s and 1970s saw more and more people visiting Gerlach to take advantage of the hot springs. (Nevada Historical Society wa00918.)

A portion of the National Geographic television special *The Haunted West* was filmed in Gerlach in March 1972. The episode is narrated by Leslie Nielsen and was first broadcast on CBS on April 12, 1973. The segment features the women of Gerlach operating a fire truck and putting out a structure fire. Helen (left) and Jewel Speelman are the women waving from the back of the truck. (Patricia Speelman.)

The *Haunted West* segment states that the women operated the fire truck because the men were working too far from town to respond quickly. Legend has it that the scene of the burning building was staged. The 1950s era truck held 300 gallons of water, which was only enough to fight a fire for about 10 minutes. (Patricia Speelman.)

In this image, Helen Speelman waves at the camera with the film crew next to her. The Gerlach segment starts with Western Pacific Railroad selling the land to the residents for $18,000. The *Reno Evening Gazette* first reported that the residents were considering buying the town in 1965, and the deal finally closed in 1975. (Patricia Speelman.)

Loella Sweet is pictured here driving the Washoe County volunteer fire department truck. Sweet owned the Gerlach Hotel that was later used in the film *Far from Home*. Today, with a population between 100 and 200, Gerlach continues to operate a volunteer fire department that also provides ambulance services to the Black Rock Desert region. (Patricia Speelman.)

In the late 1970s or early 1980s, the Inner Tube Rodeo occurred in the Black Rock Desert. Participants folded themselves inside truck inner tubes and then rolled across the desert. This event made excellent use of the extremely flat surface of the desert and would be difficult to do anywhere else. (John Bogard.)

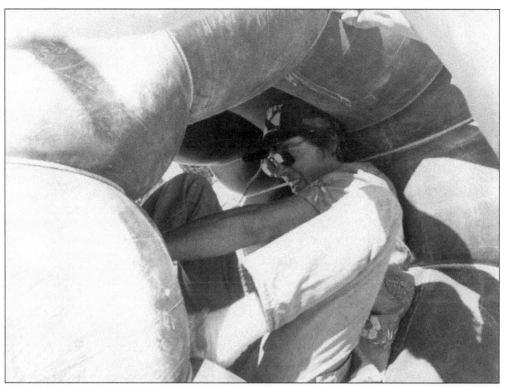

Here, John Bogard prepares to take a ride inside the tube. In the 1970s and 1980s, Bogard was a key participant in a number of unusual events on the playa. In the late 1970s, Bogard started Planet X Pottery, which he still operates today with his wife, Rachel. (John Bogard.)

One of the Coyote Dunes is in the foreground of this image with Old Razorback in the background. In 1963, Coyote Spring was measured as flowing at one gallon per minute. The Coyote Dunes had a greater flow until an artesian well was drilled at the Garrett Ranch (aka Frog Pond) in the 1950s. (John Bogard.)

Bruno Selmi and his grandson Willey Bruno Courtney are pictured here after a successful deer hunt in the 1980s. Selmi arrived in the area from Italy in 1946, worked at the Empire Gypsum plant and, in 1952, bought a Gerlach bar for $6,500. Selmi and his family own and operate Bruno's Country Club, a gas station and motel. In 2013, at the age of 89, Selmi continues to regularly tend bar. (Bruno Selmi.)

Patricia Kelley's March 1978 image of the Gerlach playground at the Gerlach Hot Springs captures the sometimes haunted beauty of the area. Gerlach has had a school for many years. The graduating class from Gerlach High School in 2011 was the largest in a decade—ten students. The school continues to operate after the 2011 mine closure. (Patricia Kelley.)

Fly Geyser, pictured here in March 1978, was created by leaks from a 1,000-foot-deep geothermal well drilled in 1964. Despite the fact that Fly Geyser is on private property, images of Fly Geyser have won several awards over the years, including one that was part of a 2010 Nevada tourism campaign. Fly Geyser is roughly 12 feet high and changes from year to year. (Patricia Kelley.)

This March 1978 image of the roughly 15-foot-tall geothermal deposit known as the Thumb, located at Fly Ranch, captures the area at a windless moment. At times, the area has 30 to 40 pools, and the springs are reported to be the largest in northwestern Nevada. The surface water is used for irrigation. (Patricia Kelley.)

This March 1978 photograph of the Thumb is markedly different from the 1940s image on the cover. It is thought that Fly Ranch is geothermally active because of the intersection between a north-south fault that extends from Winnemucca Lake to High Rock with an east-west fault that terminates at the north end of the Granite Range. (Patricia Kelley.)

This late-1930s truck was photographed on the Black Rock Desert in June 1979. Over time, vehicles like this have been seen as trash and removed by individuals with good intentions. It is sometimes difficult to differentiate between trash and a historic object. Certainly, newer abandoned vehicles should be addressed, but older abandoned vehicles may tell a part of the story of the region. (Patricia Kelley.)

Six

THE BLACK ROCK AS AN ARTISTIC MEDIUM

During the 1980s, several key events occurred on the Black Rock Desert playa that brought the region national and international notice.

The October 4, 1983, setting of a land speed record by a British team lead by Richard Noble put Gerlach on the map. Noble drove *Thrust2* to set the record at 633.468 miles per hour, which was determined from the average of two runs within one hour. Noble and his team returned to the area in 1997 to break the sound barrier with *ThrustSSC*.

In the summer of 1986, the movie *Far from Home*, starring Drew Barrymore and Matt Frewer, was filmed in the area. While the movie was not widely distributed, it did include scenes of Gerlach and the desert.

On Labor Day weekend in 1987, Mel Lyons and John Bogard produced "Croquet X Machina," a croquet game played with trucks used as mallets and nearly six-foot-diameter croquet balls. For this event, participants paid a small fee, wore white coveralls with colored hard hats, and played croquet in a unique manner. This event is likely the first organized and documented non-traditional participatory art event on the desert.

In 1989, Lyons and Bogard organized another event called "Ya Gotta Regatta—The Breakwind Dance," at which attendees had to participate by bringing wind-driven art. The annual Burning Man event continues this tradition of "no spectators" in the 1990s and beyond.

In addition to these large events, Gerlach-area photographers such as Tony Diebold and Sunny DeForest captured unique images of the area. DeWayne Williams continued to expand Guru Road, which is a mile-long series of installations annotated with words carved into rocks. Visitors continued to enjoy the Gerlach Hot Springs, prompting the citizens of Gerlach to build a swimming pool. All of these activities illustrate the artistic efforts of individuals and groups in the region.

Between 1970 and the early 1990s, DeWayne "Dooby" Williams created a collection of installations and signs known as Guru Road or Dooby Lane. Pictured is a teepee topped with skulls. The signs consist of aphorisms carved into local rocks. Williams, a US Marine, was in Japan just after the end of World War II and used his art to illustrate his views on war. (Christopher Hylands.)

In this 1980s photograph, Lloyd Mosley is standing behind one of Dooby's trees. In the 1990s, Pulitzer Prize–winning poet Gary Snyder worked with students of University of Nevada professor Peter Goin to create a limited-edition book, *Dooby Lane: A Testament Inscribed in Stone Tablets by DeWayne Williams*. This rare book sells for $1,000 per copy. (Patricia Kelley.)

In 1982, Johnny Limbo and the Smoke Creek Irregulars cut a 45-rpm record. The view on the cover, created by Brian Covey, looks northward and shows John Bogard holding on to a sign in the Black Rock Desert with the Calico Mountains in the background. The signposts were initially used for gunnery range signs and later repurposed for a variety of humorous signs. The posts were removed sometime in the first decade of the 21st century. (John Bogard.)

THIS RECORD IS DEDICATED TO ALL THE IRREGULARS WHERE-EVER THEY MIGHT BE ....

Bozo Recording · Lakeview, Oregon
Engineered by Billy Barnett & Marlin Martindale
January 1982

Guitars   —   MARTINDALE, BARNETT, LIMBO
Harmonica, Vocals — LIMBO
Bass   —   MARTINDALE
Drums   —   BARNETT
Refreshment   —   Budweiser
Cover Photo   —   Mary Leonard
Art Work   —   Brian "Gizmo" Covey
Inspiration   —   ledgendary GOATS & Bev's Juke box

A **PLANET X** Production

copyright   johnny limbo   1982

The back of the record lists the performers. Brian Covey arrived in Gerlach in the 1970s and retired from the Washoe County road crew about 30 years later. Covey produced a number of graphic art pieces for the area in the form of T-shirts and bumper stickers. (John Bogard and Brian Covey.)

As part of the Johnny Limbo project, this bus was converted in a 24-foot stage with backdrop in June 1982. Brian Covey is shown painting the backdrop, which depicts the Black Rock Desert. A number of animals from Planet X are shown; presumably, the chickens were coaxed to participate with grain. (Patricia Kelley.)

John Bogard acquired this 1938 International Harvester D-400 truck for use as a bus for the band. This August 1983 photograph shows the back of the 35-foot-long truck with the words "Beklab Electronics, Mobile Laboratory" on the side. This vehicle, or one just like it, was used by Levi Strauss & Co. as a 1939 World's Fair exhibit called "Levi's Puppet Rodeo." (Patricia Kelley.)

This August 1983 image shows the International Harvester truck being towed with Black Rock Point and King Lear Peak in the background. The previous owner was Joe Selmi (owner of Joe's Club in Gerlach). The vehicle sat for many years at Selmi's Ranch near the three-mile entrance to the playa before being purchased by John Bogard. Bogard sold it to an Auburn, California, resident who collects travel trailers. (Patricia Kelley.)

In August 1983, the Johnny Limbo and the Smoke Creek Irregulars band bus was used in a promotional photograph. Pictured here are, from left to right, Mary Bogard, Patricia Kelly, unidentified, and Sara Bogard. John Bogard (as Johnny Limbo) is on top of the truck (with the guitar) while Brian Covey is unplugging the guitar cord. (Patricia Kelley.)

In this September 1983 photograph, Sara Bogard dances on the Black Rock Desert playa with Old Razorback in the background at left. The roughly 200-square-mile flat surface makes the desert a stage almost without borders. However, the alkali chemicals found in the surface can be hard on bare feet. (Patricia Kelley.)

This September 1983 evening bonfire generates black smoke. Today, the Bureau of Land Management requires that fires be contained in raised platforms so as to prevent burn scars of discolored earth from appearing later. At the time this photograph was taken, there was so little use of the playa that evidence of visits quickly disappeared. (Patricia Kelley.)

John Bogard is pictured here in August 1985 with his *Armageddon* artwork. This panel incorporates the cracked, dried mud motif of the playa. This work illustrates a trilobite-like creature escaping an impact crater. Bogard continues to work with ceramics, and his recent work includes watercolor landscapes of the area. (Patricia Kelley.)

This c. 1981 image of a dust storm on the Black Rock Desert was used during the permit process for the 1982 *Thrust2* land speed record. This image was used to illustrate that dust storms had previously occurred on the desert. The dust cloud could be a haboob, which is a cloud of dust that is pushed in front of a thunderstorm. (Tony Diebold.)

John Ackroyd (left) and Richard Noble stand in the Black Rock Desert in this 1983 image. Ackroyd designed the *Thrust2* jet-powered car, which Noble drove to break the land speed record on October 4, 1983, with a speed of 633.468 miles per hour (the average of two runs within an hour). Noble's team returned in 1997 and broke the sound barrier with *ThrustSSC*, which traveled at an average speed of 763.035 miles per hour. (Sunny DeForest.)

Glynne Bowsher (left), an unidentified man, and Richard Noble (right) stand next to the *Thrust2* car. *Thrust2* was powered by a Rolls-Royce Avon 302 jet engine from an English Electric Lightning aircraft that developed about 30,000 horsepower. The engine consumed a gallon of fuel per second when the afterburner was lit, and the vehicle's fuel economy was about one-tenth of a mile per gallon. (Sunny DeForest.)

Thrust2 weighed about four tons, and because the playa surface is soft, the vehicle used solid, forged aluminum wheels without rubber tires. There was concern that the tracks would permanently scar the desert, but the first dust storm removed most of the tracks, and winter storms finished the job. (Tony Diebold.)

Since the *Thrust2* was a British car, the driver sat on the right side. *Thrust2* was unusual in that the left side had a passenger compartment, which was sometimes occupied on low-speed runs. The cost of the project was about $1.5 million, and the logos of the sponsors appeared on the car. (Sunny DeForest.)

To set a land speed record, the car must run in both directions within an hour, and the average of the two runs is used. After a one trip at a speed of 622.837 miles per hour, the return trip was aborted because of a fuel problem (it turned out that there was air in the line). The solution was to bleed the fuel line between runs. Here, *Thrust2* is shown starting a run. (Tony Diebold.)

The timing stands were no closer than a quarter-mile to the track. The metal wheels made ruts in the surface, so the track consisted of 16 individual tracks each 50 feet wide. The 13-mile track consisted of a measured mile in the middle with six miles on either end. The track was cleared of foreign debris that could harm the wheels or engine. (Tony Diebold.)

The dust trail represents lost energy that is unavailable to propel *Thrust2*. Dust that accumulated inside the rims was carefully cleaned out between runs so as to avoid wheel-balance problems. Dust was also hard on electronics and mechanisms. While driving, Richard Noble breathed bottled air in case of dust, fire, or canopy loss. (Tony Diebold.)

Unusual gatherings have been happening on the Black Rock Desert for many years. Over Labor Day weekend in 1987, Mel Lyons and John Bogard produced a croquet game called "Croquet X Machina," which was held with nearly six-foot-diameter balls. The event is covered in an April 11, 1988, *Sports Illustrated* article that describes the game as being played by six teams on a course that was 1,100 feet long. (Karen Fiene.)

Trucks were used as mallets for the long shots in the "Croquet X Machina" game. The trucks had inner tubes, covered with canvas, mounted on the front grill as protection for both the trucks and the croquet balls. As with regular croquet, the key was to hit the ball with the appropriate force. (Karen Fiene.)

The balls tended to move with the wind, so a team member would steady the ball in place and release it just as the truck hit the ball. "Winter Rules" were in effect, which meant that team members could stop the ball if the official determined that wind was changing its direction. (Karen Fiene.)

For safety reasons, trucks were not permitted near the wickets, so a plywood battering ram was used for the short shots through the 22-foot-tall wickets. The wickets themselves were made of PVC pipe with concrete-filled tire bases. No holes were dug in the playa. Participants paid $50 each to partially cover the expenses that included jumpsuits, color-coded hard hats, and the croquet balls. (Karen Fiene.)

The blue team executed the best shot of the day with a 75-yard downwind shot that curved into the yellow ball and put blue in place for the victory. The yellow team came in second. The yellow ball is pictured here with Old Razorback (aka "Sleeping Elephant") in the background. (Karen Fiene.)

Diane Burk stands next to the black team's Dodge Power Wagon with "Black Whole" emblazoned on either side. During play, this vehicle frequently had a rider on the roof rack to aid with alignment and strategy. Each team had a clipboard with a map of the playing field for planning purposes. (Patricia Kelley.)

In addition to bad brakes, this 1970s International Harvester garbage truck also had a bald tire, which proved not to be a significant problem in such a huge, flat area. The truck was equipped with shovels and brooms that were presumably used to clean up after the event. Today, visitors realize that "leave no trace" is at best an ideal, as many desert activities leave persistent evidence. (Patricia Kelley.)

This 1950 F-3 Ford truck, sold as the Step-N-Serve, was part of a limited production run of 2,500. The side has "Scorpion Springs Leatherworks" written on it. This vehicle was not used as a mallet in the croquet game. The shade structure of this camp was erected without digging holes in the playa surface. (Patricia Kelley.)

In this panoramic shot of the "Croquet X Machina" event, the sheer scale of the amount of open space becomes apparent. This image is also reminiscent of the images of wagons crossing the desert during *The Winning of Barbara Worth*. Much of the haze is from the California-Oregon forest fires known as "The Siege of 1987." (Patricia Kelley.)

In the summer of 1988, the town of Gerlach was the primary location for the Drew Barrymore/ Matt Frewer movie *Far from Home*. Gerlach's paved main street was covered with gravel for the filming, a reminder of one of the town slogans: "Where the pavement ends and the West begins." (Cindy Carter.)

The Palomino Guest Ranch Trailer Park set for *Far from Home* included an aboveground swimming pool that was used in a scene featuring Drew Barrymore. The plot of the movie is that a father and daughter are stranded in the town of Banco, where a series of murders occurs. (Cindy Carter.)

In the summer of 1988, a false front was added to 390 Main Street for the movie *Far from Home*. The interior shots of the store murder scene were filmed elsewhere, at the Empire store. This building, then known as the old post office, now serves as the Burning Man office. (Cindy Carter.)

The Gerlach Hotel, owned by Loella Sweet, is featured in *Far from Home*. In the movie, the building is the trailer park office. Legend has it that the porch was deliberately built in a crooked manner for the film, but the hotel is built on top of several hot springs, so the ground may have shifted over time. (Cindy Carter.)

In 1989, Mel Lyons and John Bogard used this postcard to invite participants to "Ya Gotta Regatta—The Breakwind Dance." The reverse reads, "Let's get this straight! You and yours are invited to bring a kinetic sculpture of your own design that moves by the power of the wind to the Black Rock Desert over Labor Day weekend." This event was the playa's first documented, formal bring-your-own-art event. (Mel Lyons and Karen Fiene.)

YA GOTTA REGATTA —
THE BREAKWIND DANCE

Brian Covey (aka Gizmo), who was working with the Washoe County road crew, created this metal strap sphere—with hard hats as paddles—in which the sphere rotated in the wind like a waterwheel. The piece now resides at Planet X Pottery a few miles west of Gerlach. (Karen Fiene.)

Mel Lyons's piece *The Fallacy of Logic* recreated the chess match in *Alice in Wonderland*. The chessboard is pictured at left, and the Queen of Hearts' chess pieces are at right. Both the chessboard and the queen's pieces were let loose with the wind, and some of them traveled for miles. (Karen Fiene.)

The chessboard was nicknamed "Wind Wall" and consisted of blue tarps mounted on small wheels. The "Wind Wall" pieces were not as stable in the wind as chess pieces. On most days in the summer, the wind becomes stronger throughout the day and tends to weaken at sunset. (Karen Fiene.)

The Queen of Hearts' chess pieces consisted of ripstop nylon fabric on bicycle wheels with hard hats, perhaps repurposed from the earlier work at this location. Some of the chess pieces were found downwind after having collided with each other in some sort of symbolic chess battle. The larger wheels and smaller fabric area helped make these pieces stable. (Karen Fiene.)

This picture of Ruth ? from August 1981 illustrates the sort of visitor who frequented Gerlach Hot Springs. In 1973, a 19-year-old woman died at the springs when she mistakenly dove into one of the boiling pools during a late-night visit. Today, the property is privately owned, and the springs are not generally in use. (Patricia Kelley.)

This August 1988 photograph shows Brian Covey's sign at the peak of the bathhouse at the Gerlach "Great Boiling" Springs. Like much of Covey's work, the sign is indicative of his wry sense of humor and way with words. The bathhouse walls were constructed of old railroad ties, a common material used for buildings in Gerlach. (Patricia Kelley.)

In the 1980s the community decided that creating a separate pool for residents and visitors would improve safety and bring tourism to the area. The selected location was between the springs proper and the edge of town. Mary Bogard (right) is pictured here in October 1984 installing concrete reinforcing mesh for the bottom of the swimming pool. (Patricia Kelley.)

In October 1984, the concrete was poured for the bottom of the Gerlach swimming pool. The New Gerlach Hot Springs Committee was led by Wanda Heiss, Sunny (Schatz) DeForest, Joan Iraoqui, Kathy Adams, and Linda Campbell. The project was paid for via community fundraising and built with volunteer labor. (Patricia Kelley.)

In 1989, the New Gerlach Hot Springs Committee built this bathhouse at the edge of town. Unfortunately, the health department would not provide it with a permit because the water filters were being plugged by sediment. As a result, the bathhouse and pool have rarely, if ever, been open. (Sunny DeForest.)

Golfing on the playa sometimes presented a problem when the cup was 700 yards from the pin. Photographer Douglas Keister came to the Black Rock Desert in 1981 and started golfing on the desert in 1988. The event grew into an amateur golf tournament called the Black Rock Self Invitational Golf Tournament at Lucifer's Anvil Golf Course. (Douglas Keister.)

Douglas Keister's 1990 book, *Black Rock: Portraits of the Playa,* was the first modern art book about the playa. Keister realized the potential of the playa "as the world's largest stage, Nothing but Earth and sky," and decided to do a book. Keister would invite friends to his Emeryville, California, studio, where they would plan the shots. A group would then travel to the playa and take the photographs. (Douglas Keister.)

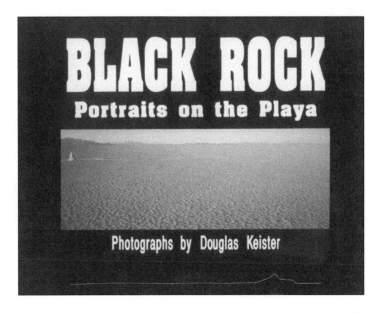

This image from Douglas Keister's *Black Rock: Portraits of the Playa* is captioned "Roberto Varriale, Locals viewing recently transplanted Italians in the Black Rock Desert. Thanks to Laura, Marina, Paola, Betti and Paolo." The evening view looks north with the Black Rock in the far distance at left. A closer look suggests that the wind did not lessen at sunset on this day. (Douglas Keister.)

The fine-grained mud of the dry lakebed itself has been used as a prop. In this image from *Black Rock: Portraits of the Playa*, Rachel (left), Maggie (center), and Judy Houck are pictured as entrepreneurs. One of the Coyote Dunes is shown on the left, with the Selenite Range in the background at right. (Douglas Keister.)

John Bogard (left) and Brian Covey (center) are pictured here in land yachts on the Black Rock Desert. The flat expanse of the dry lakebed has attracted many unique activities. The Sunny Acres Sipping and Sailing Society held its regatta on the Black Rock Desert for many years. Changes in the surface of the desert prompted them to move to a different dry lakebed in 2005. (Douglas Keister.)

There is a wide variety of land yachts; this one from 1988 appears to have three separate wing-masts that form an airfoil. Unlike regular waterborne sailboats, land yachts and iceboats can go faster than the wind. As of 2013, the land yacht speed record was set in 2009 at Ivanpah, Nevada, with a speed of 126.1 miles per hour in a wind of 30–50 miles per hour. (Patricia Kelley).

Tony Diebold is shown on his horse Chap with his border collie Critter in December 1989. Diebold's career includes photographs of the land speed record that appear in a book by National Geographic. In 2013, Diebold's line of work included guiding hunters in the Black Rock and other areas. (R'Deen Diebold.)

These large ice crystals formed on the playa during pogonip in January 1986. It is hard to get a sense of scale in this alien-looking landscape, but the crystals are many inches across. The dune in the background appears to have footprints on it. This image is one of two images that show the type of dunes that started appearing in 2000. (Tony Diebold.)

Most people visit the Black Rock Region during the summer, though hunters are present in the spring and fall. The beauty of the winter is mostly witnessed by locals. This November 1983 southward view shows the US Gypsum plant at Empire in the distance on the right, the Granite Ranch in the near foreground, and the town of Gerlach and the Gerlach Hot Springs at left. (Tony Diebold.)

This November 1985 view of Old Razorback shows a world untouched by humankind. Gerlach gets an average of 7.46 inches of liquid precipitation per year, which includes the liquid from an average of 11.5 inches of snow. (The amount of liquid in one inch of snow is not always equal to one inch of rain and varies.) A common definition of a desert is a region that receives less than 10 inches of precipitation annually, so Gerlach—like most of Nevada—is considered to be desert. (Tony Diebold.)

This 1990 photograph taken by Peter Goin is titled *Moonrise over Black Rock*. Goin took the photograph with Ansel Adams's *Moonrise, Hernandez, New Mexico* (1941) in mind. In the book *Black Rock*, written with Paul F. Starrs, Goin writes that it was happenstance that Adams was in the right place at the right time. However, Goin, knowing the area and having viewed the Black Rock hundreds—if not thousands—of times, waited for moonrise to "embody the essence of this place." *Black Rock*, published in 2005, provides an excellent, in-depth overview of the area, including the time period covered by this book as well as events after 1990. Goin's work in the area from the 1980s to the 2000s illustrates the time period ranging from when the area first started to get noticed to when concerns about overuse became national news. Goin is a faculty member in the art department at the University of Nevada, Reno. (Peter Goin.)

BIBLIOGRAPHY

Ackroyd, John. *Just for the Record: Thrust 2*. Middlesex, England: CHW Roles, 1984.

Barrymore, Drew and Todd Gold. *Little Girl Lost*. New York: Pocket, 1990.

Boettger, Susan. *Earthworks: Art and the Landscape of the Sixties*. Berkeley: University of California Press, 2008.

Bonham, Harold F. Jr., Larry J. Garside, Richard B. Jones, Keith G. Papke, Jay Quade, and Joseph V. Tingle. *A Mineral Inventory of the Paradise-Denio and Sonoma-Gerlach Resource Areas, Winnemucca District, Nevada*. Reno: Nevada Bureau of Mines and Geology, 1985.

Bruff, Joseph Goldsborough, Georgia Willis Read, and Ruth Gaines. *Gold Rush: The Journals, Drawings, and Other Papers of J. Goldsborough Bruff, Captain, Washington City and California Mining Association, April 2, 1849–July 20, 1851*. New York: Columbia University Press, 1949.

Curran, Harold. *Fearful Crossing: The Central Overland Trail Through Nevada*. Reno: Nevada Publications, 1987.

Earl, Phillip I. "Hollywood Comes to the Black Rock: The Story of the Making of *The Winning of Barbara Worth*." *North Central Nevada Historical Society* (Winter 1988): 3–20.

Elliott, Russell R. and William D. Rowley. *History of Nevada*. Lincoln: University of Nebraska Press, 1987.

Fairfield, Asa Merrill. *Fairfield's Pioneer History of Lassen County, California*. San Francisco: H.S. Crocker, 1916.

Goin, Peter and Paul F. Starrs. *Black Rock*. Reno: University of Nevada Press, 2005.

Goldsmith, Oliver. *Overland in Forty-Nine: The Recollections of a Wolverine Ranger After a Lapse of Forty-Seven Years*. Detroit: self-published, 1896.

Keister, Douglas. *Black Rock: Portraits on the Playa*. Emeryville: California Photo Service, 1990.

Klamath County Historical Society. *Applegate Trail*. Klamath Falls, OR: Klamath County Historical Society, 1971.

Rumsey, David. *The David Rumsey Historical Map Collection*. http://www.davidrumsey.com.

Schulmerich, Alma. *Josie Pearl*. Salt Lake City: Deseret Book Co., 1963.

Swartzlow, Ruby Johnson. *Lassen: His Life and Legacy*. Loomis, CA: Loomis Museum, 1964.

Wheeler, Sessions. *The Black Rock Desert*. Caldwell, ID: Caxton Press, 1978.

INDEX

Visit us at
arcadiapublishing.com

CPSIA information can be obtained
at www.ICGtesting.com
Printed in the USA
BVHW012206161221
624262BV00003B/28